The
ROOMING
HOUSE
MILLIONAIRE

The ROOMING HOUSE MILLIONAIRE

Investing Out of the Box for **Maximum Profit**

HENRY VILA

A catalogue record for this book is available from the National Library of Australia

Printed in Australia by McPherson's Printing
Project management by Michael Hanrahan Publishing
Cover and layout design by G Sharp Design, LLC.
www.gsharpmajor.com

ISBN 978-1-923007-92-5

This book has been created by humans without the assistance of artificial intelligence.

Disclaimer
The material in this publication is of the nature of general comment only, and does not represent professional advice. It is not intended to provide specific guidance for particular circumstances and it should not be relied on as the basis for any decision to take action or not take action on any matter which it covers. Readers should obtain professional advice where appropriate, before making any such decision. To the maximum extent permitted by law, the author and associated entities and publisher disclaim all responsibility and liability to any person, arising directly or indirectly from any person taking or not taking action based on the information in this publication.

C O N T E N T S

INTRODUCTION

WHEN IT COMES to wealth creation and investing, the Holy Grail is financial freedom. This means different things to different people but, generally, financial freedom is the idea that we will some day, in the very near future, arrive at a point where we are enjoying the unlimited delights of passive income and we can finally live the life of our dreams.

If you were to take a leisurely stroll through the business and finance section at your local bookstore on any Saturday afternoon, you would find hundreds of books making this exact promise, whether through property investing, mastering the stock market, or creating a lucrative side hustle.

The problem is—most of it is bullshit!

These various prescriptions for financial freedom often have two glaring problems:

1. faulty assumptions about the journey
2. faulty assumptions about the destination.

FAULTY ASSUMPTIONS ABOUT THE JOURNEY

The world is full of people proposing various systems for creating the life of your dreams through passive income. Passive income is the 'how' or the fuel that will be used to reach the destination—financial freedom! It is the promise that you will be able to invest in something or create something that delivers truckloads of cash on a regular basis while you sip mojitos on the beach.

The problem with passive income is it's almost never passive! It may be possible if you have a big fat trust fund where even a safe investment could create endless cash flow, but what about the rest of us?

You could create a business, but creating a business consumes even more time and energy than being an employee. The business owner needs to become an expert in more than just the thing they are trained in or want to offer as a product or service. They need to be a marketer, salesperson, administrator, operations expert, accountant and so much more. Starting and running a business is never passive.

You could invest in the stock market, but that's not passive either. You need to understand the markets and the economy, as well as the individual companies that you are investing in. And even if you get that right, an unfounded rumour can wipe years' worth of growth from your portfolio and you can't do anything to influence the outcome. Investing in the stock market is certainly not passive, and can also be scary. Even if you choose to invest in a low-maintenance index fund, you still need to do your homework to choose the right fund manager and track their performance versus fees and other costs.

Perhaps you've thought that property investing is the answer. But it's far from passive either. Again, you need to know your market to find a suitable property, and then need to gather the deposit and find a lender so you can secure it. You need to make any renovations required to attract a tenant. Once you have the tenant, you need to manage ongoing fees and maintenance, all while hoping the interest rate doesn't go up too much and your tenant keeps paying on time. Property is never passive.

I came to these various realisations myself over many years.

I grew up in Venezuela and trained as a systems engineer. After about four years in the corporate world, I started my own business during the dotcom frenzy of the late 1990s. That went well until the dotcom crash of 2001, and so I returned to the corporate world. The economy in Venezuela wasn't great at the time, and it wasn't much better in the United States, so I was on the lookout for a new place to call home. I had a friend who lived in Australia and he suggested I join him 'Down Under'. At the time, all I knew about Australia was that it was also home to a lot of kangaroos. On further investigation, I found a buoyant economy and an engineering skills shortage. My visa application was accepted so I moved to Melbourne to continue my career in the corporate world for the next 15 or so years. I completed my MBA and climbed the corporate ladder, eventually switching into high paying consultancy work with blue chip companies.

I loved my job, but in what would be the last year of my employment I realised that I had been away from home 220 nights out of 365—more than half the year! At the time, my twin boys were just three years old and I vividly remember leaving to go to the airport again and saying goodbye to them. It was clear they didn't really understand what was going on. They didn't seem to realise that I lived with them, and instead thought I was just visiting. It broke my heart. I didn't want them growing up thinking their dad just visited them now and again. I realised my job, and what it required from me, wasn't sustainable. I wasn't being the husband I wanted to be and I wasn't able to be the father I wanted to be. In a matter of weeks, I went from loving my job to hating it—and desperate to find a way out.

Like many others, I had been investing in property while I was employed, and I had assumed that property would offer me a way to reduce my tax bill in the short term and build wealth over the long term. But I began to see it doesn't always work like that. I certainly met many people who believed the myth and bought several investment properties, only to find that they became even more of a wage slave. Far from gaining more freedom, they were even more trapped in their job because it was their salary that covered the costs when things went wrong—such as interest rates going up again or a tenant trashing the property. On top of doing a full-time job (and even with a property manager), they were having to manage plumber visits and carpet installers. If property was supposed to deliver freedom—it didn't feel like it.

But I was still sure that property was my answer, so I left my job and went into property investment full-time. At first, I did what a lot of others were doing. I bought blocks of land and built two or three townhouses and then sold them. I loved it, and it certainly delivered more perceived freedom. I learned that I could make money without being employed but, in truth, I had just swapped one job with another. I wasn't away from home for hundreds of nights a year anymore but I was still working very long hours. And it certainly wasn't passive income. It was a tonne of work and once I sold the properties, I had to repeat the process all over again to make more money.

It became very clear to me that growing my portfolio in the traditional way was never going to give me the financial freedom I was looking for. I realised I could either find another job and continue to use my newly minted property investing skills to build wealth, but not really gain much freedom, or I could look for a different type of property investment strategy that would give me the freedom and the cash flow.

Spoiler alert: I opted for the second option. But before I explain what that was, let's look at the second problem with our obsession with financial freedom.

FAULTY ASSUMPTIONS ABOUT THE DESTINATION

The issue here is that most people have a fundamental lack of understanding or clarity about their destination. Regardless of the route, the destination is always some sort of mythical (but vague) 'financial freedom'. In my mind, I always see becoming financially free as similar to a cyclist crossing the finish line of the Tour de France, arms raised over their head in wild jubilation.

That's bullshit too.

What so many of the authors and seminar presenters fail to appreciate is that everyone is different. What I wanted to achieve when I was still a consultant was very different to what I want to achieve now. When I was a consultant and unhappy in my job, all I cared about was being able to quit my job. Today, I probably work harder than I've ever worked in my life but I also feel more freedom! It's all relative and what we want changes as we change.

According to conventional wisdom, what you need to do is work out how much money you currently spend every year, add a little extra for contingency and, when your investments are creating income that passes that number, voila—you are financially free. Mojitos all around.

That makes no sense. Firstly, it doesn't acknowledge that everyone is different with different goals. If your goal is to quit your job so you and your young family can buy a campervan and take a three-year trip around Australia, your needs are very different to the couple who want to buy matching Mercedes and travel business class to exotic destinations five times a year.

And, secondly, it also creates a very, very high bar that stops people from doing anything.

Say you wanted to replace your $100,000 a year salary and are thinking of buying an investment property to do so. Even if you don't know very much about property, you will already have some sense of how much properties cost in your area. If you pay rent, you will know the going rate. This knowledge might allow you to do a 'back of the envelope' calculation to work out you could clear $1000 a month from a potential property, or $12,000 a year. You'd need to buy nine similar properties to give you an income of $108,000 a year. If you have never bought a single property in your life, or you've only ever bought your family home, how likely is that? Are we honestly suggesting that you can magically conjure up the courage and financial resources to buy nine properties? It's completely unrealistic—and sets people up for failure.

I've lost count of the number of people I've spoken to about property investing who believe that they have missed the boat. If only they had bought in the 70s, 80s, 90s or even 2000s, they tell me, they would be free and clear now. Or the people who have told me that property investing for ordinary people is finished because interest rates are never going to be so low again. Those are valid arguments and they sound plausible, but they assume that the traditional way to invest in property is the *only* way to invest in property.

It's not the only way—but it took me a while to realise it! I stuck with the traditional approach for a few years. But at night when

I couldn't sleep, I kept wondering, 'What if I wake up one day and hate this work too?' I had been surprised by how quickly I went from loving my consultancy role to hating it, and I was worried that in five or ten years' time I might stop loving property. Besides—I still wasn't creating freedom over the long term.

What I needed was the ability to do more with less, and to hang on to each property after completion so collectively they created an income over time. But I realised building townhouses was pointless. I needed to build something more innovative. One of the fascinating cultural norms of Australia is this notion of space. Australia is a truly massive country and there is a huge amount of empty space between the places people live—predominantly the towns and cities. But, certainly in the cities, people simply can't afford the space anymore.

And yet people still need somewhere to live. That's never going to change. What needs to change is our investment strategies. The old-school cookie-cutter property investment strategies that worked in the 1990s just don't work anymore. (More on why in chapter 2.) To be fair, these strategies might still work for the top 1 per cent of income earners, but they certainly don't work for everyone else. Plus, those strategies don't work for society. Housing is a major issue for just about every developed nation and yet we are still largely building, buying and selling the same types of properties. It makes no sense.

As a result, far too many young people are being forced to live in shabby shared accommodation or poor-quality housing on the outer edges of the cities. And older people who no longer want to rattle around in the family home once the children have left have too few options. They realise they want (or need) to sell, but don't know where to go. People are basically being priced out of cities all over the world. I grew up in Venezuela and space was not something we took for granted. I've also spent a lot of time in New York, where everyone lives in apartments, sometimes in spaces smaller than the average Australian garage. Places such as Hong Kong and Singapore have also embraced small spaces. Small spaces can be beautiful, and they are certainly easier to manage, clean and run.

It's time we rethink the large home with big garden and two-car garage. We need housing that fits various stages of our lives. We need small options for when we are starting out on our professional careers or starting out in a relationship, and larger when the relationship turns serious and we start to raise a family. We then need small again as we move into older age and the family have flown the nest. Who wants to be cleaning a four-bedroom house in their 70s anyway?

THE ROOMING HOUSE REVOLUTION

The investment model I use now is investing in next-generation rooming houses. Chances are, as soon as you read the phrase 'rooming house' you panicked! When I speak to clients about this type of investment, they invariably remember examples from when they were growing up—a dodgy old pub, perhaps, where all the local alcoholics lived upstairs, or a rundown old house that had been converted to rooms that housed the mentally unstable, local drug dealers and habitually unemployed!

I could have sanitised the language and called them micro-apartments or multi-dwelling residences, or come up with some other clever term to avoid the negative associations most people have about rooming houses. Many people in this investment space employ this exact tactic for that very reason. But I'm aiming for a no-bullshit guide so let's just call it what it is and rehabilitate the term instead.

Forget everything you ever thought you knew about rooming houses. This investment strategy is focused on next-generation rooming houses—that is, a collection of high-quality, purpose-built individual studios inside a single property. A communal entrance leads to private individual studios with their own bathroom, kitchenette, living and sleeping space, outside seating area or balcony. And I'm going to show you how to tap into this growing investment trend. Today, this is the only type of property I own apart from my family home.

And, best of all, this is not a strategy for the already wealthy. Most of my clients are 'mum and dad' investors in their 40s or 50s who recognise that traditional investing via property or the stock market is not going to deliver the returns they need. Some of my clients are people who already own assets that are not performing or who have a sizeable superannuation fund but are not convinced it's going to see them beyond 10 or 20 years. Once this investment strategy is in place, my clients are routinely generating around $50,000 a year positive cash flow per rooming house, and I have several clients who are so excited by the strategy they are building several rooming houses. What is the better outcome? Having $1 million in superannuation that offers $50,000 a year for 20 years and not much beyond (depending on market returns), or using that $1 million to create ongoing income that provides $50,000 a year forever while also helping others live in nice, clean, secure homes? I think you can work it out!

In this book, I provide all the information you need to join the rooming house revolution. In chapter 1, I explore what it means to you to be financially free so you can get a better idea of what you need to live the life you want. In chapter 2, I look under the hood of the various wealth creation options available to you, and explain why this one is the best while helping you get over any lingering unease about the idea of rooming houses. Chapter 3 onwards is dedicated to this different type of property investing, and I'll explain exactly how it's done.

The world is jam-packed with people who have a vested interest in convincing you it is possible to create passive income and gain financial freedom through some form of investment or business opportunity. This includes the banks, keen for you to borrow money, seminar providers, keen for you to buy their online or in-person programs, real estate agents, keen on their commissions, fund managers, charging 6 per cent fees each year for doing very little, and even publishers, who want you to buy the next book on investing. And, yes, it could be argued that I am also one of those with a vested interest, but the purpose of this book is to kickstart a rooming house revolution.

I don't sell seminar tickets. I build rooming houses for clients and, if they want their investment to be truly passive, my company also offers rooming house management. That's it. But this is a strategy that anyone can do and I will explain how in this book. If you want to build your own, you can. If you want someone else to do it, there are providers, including me and my company, who can help. You don't even need the $1 million in cash to get started; you can use existing assets to secure the funding. And you will be changing the lives of your tenants for the better while you create cash flow today and secure your future.

CHAPTER 1

WHAT IS YOUR DEFINITION OF FINANCIAL FREEDOM?

IF YOU ARE reading this book, I think I can assume you are interested in investing. Perhaps, like me, you are still passionate about property but are struggling to make it work using the well-worn traditional strategies. But before I dive into why I believe that property investing (with a twist) is still the answer, let's just stop and have a closer look at your ideal destination.

What are you trying to achieve?

No-one can argue that the pandemic wasn't a global catastrophe. Far too many people lost loved ones. For those not so directly impacted, however, the pandemic delivered an unexpected silver lining. Many people had some space, often for the first time, to re-think their lives. Forced to isolate to get the virus under control, millions of people began to realise that what they thought they wanted and what they thought they needed wasn't the case at all.

Significant vested interests are determined to convince us that we need to work all the hours God sends so we can make as much money as possible, and then use that money to create financial freedom. But 'financial freedom' is never the same for two people.

As I said in the introduction, when I first started to think about financial freedom and investing, all I really knew is that I wanted to leave my job. I wasn't enjoying the long hours and the travelling, and my work was negatively affecting my quality of life and my family. And while a global pandemic was a tough reason for many of the world's population to properly assess their quality of life, the outcome has made millions of people question the way they lived before the pandemic, with very few eager to return to their pre-pandemic work–life balance.

The assumption is that financial freedom will increase your quality of life. This is a logical and valid assumption. If you have enough money to live on without having to work, you can be liberated from the tyranny of work and can spend your life doing the things you really want to do.

But most of us haven't considered what we really want to do. In my own case, I didn't know what I wanted—I just knew what I didn't want. I didn't want to be a consultant anymore. Once I'd quit that job, what I wanted changed again. And what I considered to be financial freedom changed again.

I am now in the position where I could retire if I want to, but I don't want to. I love what I'm doing and work doesn't feel like a grind. Of course, I still have tough days but, overall, I'm loving life. I don't want to play golf. I might change my mind in ten years and, if so, I can adapt my definition of financial freedom to accommodate my change of heart. Right now, though, I'm doing what I want to do. And the same can be true for you.

You don't need to have everything figured out now. You don't need to create millions to achieve financial freedom. What you need to aim for depends on what you want to achieve. And most of us can achieve freedom far faster than we imagine—if we pay attention to what will make us happy.

And social science has already proven that what makes us happy is not money. In a now famous Princeton University study conducted by Daniel Kahneman and Angus Deaton, researchers found very little correlation between happiness and money, once income reached a 'comfortable' level. Using Gallup data from 450,000 Americans, they discovered that money increased happiness levels up to around US$75,000 (AUD$113,000) a year. Beyond that, more money did not deliver more happiness.[1]

Some other researchers have criticised the 2010 study, saying it is now too old to offer up relevant insights. Certainly, a later study (from 2019) found that the global happiness income was now US$160,000.[2] However, the point is, regardless of which one is more accurate, both figures are significantly lower than most of us imagine or we are told we need to be happy.

I appreciate that happiness and financial freedom are not the same thing, but we almost certainly assume that being financially free will deliver happiness. So wouldn't it make a lot more sense to work out what is going to make us happy and cost that!

In the current financial freedom debate, however, there is zero appreciation for the fact that for most people an extra $10,000 or $20,000 a year could be life-changing. It may not be sexy and it

1   Kahneman D, Deaton A (2010), 'High income improves evaluation of life but not emotional well-being' PNAS Early Edition.

2   Schools D (2019), 'I took Yale's "most popular class ever" — and it completely changed how I spend my money', CNBC Make It.

certainly won't pack out arenas or sell millions of books, but most people don't need to replace their entire income to gain significantly more freedom. Most people don't want to sit on the couch forever and binge-watch Netflix. They want to have more options and more control over their lives now, and into the future. Perhaps that extra income means you can buy that motorhome so you can go surfing at the weekend. Or perhaps that extra income allows you to cut your hours so you only work four days a week and care for your grandkids one day a week. Achieving that slight increase in income can mean you get to experience the increase in freedom you crave without having to have millions in your super pot. Or you may reach your initial goal and ramp it up. It's up to you.

We all need money. But how much we need and what it will provide for us is as unique as our thumb print. Besides, how depressing would it be to slog your guts out for decades to achieve some arbitrary amount of money, only to find out that you could have changed your life, found more freedom, and been doing something you loved decades earlier?

Financial freedom is a process and there are always degrees of freedom—each as valid as the next depending on what *you* want.

SO, WHAT DO YOU WANT?

Before we start unpacking strategies, you need to really stop and consider what you want to achieve. How much do you need to allow you to do what you want? Creating wealth is not just about how much money you accumulate, but also about how much you spend.

This is one of the quirks of financial freedom that I discovered. Once I started to make some wins with my investing, I could have stepped back, maybe trimmed my expenses a little and put my feet up, but that's not what happened for me. The more I made, the more I wanted to make—and the more my expectations and dreams grew. I noticed pretty quickly that the number that I needed to achieve to be financially free was very different from some of my friends, for example. I think part of that was because I got used to making—and also spending—a lot of money when I was a consultant. But I can change that at any time based on what I want at each stage of my life.

The same is true for you. There is no finish line when it comes to financial freedom. What that looks like will always change. Financial freedom is going to look very different for the young single adult compared to how it will look for someone with a family. It's going to look different again for someone in older age. And these differences are just based on life stage, never mind your own personality quirks and aspirations. This is why there is no right or wrong answer when it comes to what financial freedom means for you.

For me, stepping back and declaring myself financially free didn't make sense. I'm still young and, more importantly, I love what I do. I've created a business that is very fulfilling and challenging, and I'm happy to continue adding to my wealth through that business and investing in rooming houses. My family and I enjoy a nice life. It's not extravagant, although I do drive a nice car and we enjoy a few toys and regular travel—but our choices are simply our choices.

If what you want is to reduce the hours you work so you can enjoy a hobby or travel—because that's what makes your heart sing—then cost that. Use those costings as your guide, rather than some arbitrary figure plucked from the ether by someone who wants you to buy their investing course or work until you drop!

Also, wealth is not just about equity or what you own on paper. It's about income—today! It's about finding out how to create what you need or how to create the extra that you need to change your lifestyle today—not ten years from now. Understanding this can make all the different to the quality of your life—*now*!

And don't guess. Work it out.

Change the way you think about financial freedom. Instead of it being a lofty goal way out in the future, bring it closer. What can you do today that can add a few thousand a month to your income? What unnecessary expenses can you cut back on today to allow you to life your dream life, albeit part-time, now. Once you make that a reality, work on the new plan so you can work even less or you can create even more as your needs and desires change.

The COVID pandemic was horrible, with far-reaching consequences. But if it reminded us that our lives are right here, right now, then it's delivered a huge benefit to humanity.

CHAPTER 2

YOUR WEALTH CREATION OPTIONS

THE MOST POPULAR ways to create wealth are to create a business or side hustle, buy shares or invest in property. Let's run through the first two of these options, before focusing more deeply on property investing.

DRAWBACKS TO STARTING A BUSINESS OR INVESTING IN SHARES

I've created my own business, so I know nothing is easy or passive about this option. It's long hours and hard work, and that's true whether it's your full-time gig or it's a side hustle on top of your existing job. Running any business is often all-consuming. Even if you are great at what you do, as soon as you build a business around that capability, you must also become great at so many other things—including managing finances and people. And the statistics around failed business are stark.

I have a friend who started a side hustle on a well-known US creator platform. She and her business partner were convinced this was going to be their pathway to riches and 'easy street'. That was, until they noticed that the only people who seemed to be making money on the platform were the people whose business was selling courses, products or services that helped people to make money on the platform! I see this in my own industry, where plenty of people are selling courses, mentorship programs or 'inner circle' coaching on how to invest in property, instead of just investing in property. It reminds me of the adage, 'Those who can, do; those who can't, teach.'

As for shares, share investing can be a useful way to diversify a financial portfolio; however, for wealth creation, shares have two major drawbacks. First, when you buy shares in a big corporation, you have no control over how that business operates. If the company decides to upgrade their private jet, then you as a shareholder are paying for that. Unless you are someone like Warren Buffett and you have accumulated a significant shareholding in a company, you have zero control over how well that business and, therefore, the stock performs. Of course, if you had the sort of wealth that could buy enough shares in a company to warrant a seat on the board, you wouldn't be reading this book because you would already be insanely wealthy!

The other drawback with shares is the lack of leverage. If you want to invest $1 million in shares, you pretty much need to have $1 million in cash to buy those shares. (You can get what are known as 'margin loans', but these come with high interest rates, increased risk and strict conditions on what you can invest in and how much you can borrow.) That is not the case with property. You could buy a property for $1 million with far less than $1 million in cash. Borrowing money to buy property is far easier than it is when buying shares. And you can borrow far more to buy property than shares. For those two reasons alone, I focus my attention on property investing.

To me, property investing is still the best route to financial freedom—*but* not the way you might think.

OLD-SCHOOL PROPERTY INVESTING

For the past 50 years, and particularly gathering pace in the 1990s onwards, two main property investment strategies have been employed around the world, including in Australia:

1. buy, fix or subdivide, and flip
2. buy and hold.

You can find all sorts of additional strategies around how to succeed with each option, and there are different assets classes, such as commercial real estate or residential, but the vast majority of property investors are currently using one or both of these strategies. My argument is that they no longer work very well.

FOCUSING ON BUY, RENOVATE AND FLIP

Most people get into property with strategy one in mind. And to be fair, this strategy was a 'no-brainer' for decades. All the investor needed to do was find a property that was run-down or had dated decor, buy it, fit a new kitchen and/or bathroom, lay new carpets and give the whole property a fresh lick of paint. The property was then put back on the market, and sold or 'flipped' — and the investor would pocket the profit, which was often substantial. Then they could just repeat the process.

Starting in the early 2000s and right up to now, countless TV shows have tracked this type of investment. Everything from *Auction Squad* in the early 2000s to the wildly successful *The Block* were (and are) Australian favourites. In *Auction Squad*, a home owner would get a valuation for their home at the start of the program. Presenter Johanna Griggs and her 'Auction Squad', consisting of a landscaper, builder, interior designer and other 'tradies', would then transform the property in a few days. The property was then revalued, with the difference often staggering. Although not technically focused on property investing, the show certainly helped to teach home owners the value of presentation. (Ironically, this made it much harder for investors to find those run-down properties with dated decor!) *The Block*, on the other hand, is a reality TV show that charts the progress of various teams, each competing to win the profits after auction for the property they develop.

These shows and many others like them really brought property investing into the collective consciousness as a route to financial freedom. Of course, the purpose of these shows was to make good TV, not necessarily to help people make money. Shows such as *The Block* always had a final sale (and internal bickering) to create the drama. But I have yet to meet anyone who has achieved financial freedom using strategy one alone.

TRYING OUT BUY AND HOLD

Most people, including me, realise this eventually and get into the second strategy—buy and hold. I realised this after upgrading the first strategy from renovate and flip to subdivide and flip. As

I mention in the introduction, I would buy a home on a large plot, demolish the house, and build two or three townhouses in its place. I would then sell the townhouses, and I made very good money doing so. But this meant the assets were gone and I, therefore, needed to start the whole process all over again. Ironically, shows such as *The Block* also taught home owners and would-be investors that houses on huge plots of land were much more valuable than the same size property on a smaller block, making it even harder to find those plots. If you look back at a typical Australian home built in the 1950s, for example, it would likely be on 1000 square meters of land. Included would be a large garden or expansive front drive, and an even larger garden at the back. As cities and populations grew, it made sense to subdivide those excessively large plots to create more homes and more wealth. Again, however, when those subdivisions were sold the asset was gone and the investor had to start again—facing fewer options and more competition.

It became obvious to me pretty quickly that I needed to find a way to keep hold of the properties I was buying, renovating or subdividing—otherwise, I was never going to create the financial freedom I was after. And I was not the only one to arrive at that conclusion. Investors, en masse, ploughed into buy and hold. This strategy involves purchasing a property with the intention of holding onto it for the long term. The idea is that over time the property will appreciate, making it worth more than the investor paid for it. While they wait for that appreciation to happen, the investor can also generate rental income. Sounds great, but buy and hold has not been the saviour many hoped it would be.

If you invest in traditional property in Australia, the system is such that you are probably not going to create any overall income from that buy and hold property for a long time. In fact, it's probably going to turn into a cash-guzzling monster. This can be a real kick in the teeth. Investors buy a couple of buy and hold properties and, instead of these properties helping them achieve financial freedom, they find they are having to cut back on household expenses or work overtime to get more money to cover interest and other costs—and keep the monster from taking everything!

In most instances today, the achievable rent for a buy and hold property isn't even enough to cover the mortgage, certainly in those first few years, never mind the rates, water costs, strata fees, landlord insurance and maintenance. The only thing keeping this strategy alive is the fact that, in Australia at least, property has seen massive capital gains over the last 30 years or so. And this is what a vast network of professionals point to as evidence for the validity of this strategy. In essence, this network is also instrumental in keeping this strategy alive because it serves their vested interests. Everyone in the supply chain of traditional property investment—from real estate agents making commission on the sale to the tax accountants charging fees to the banks collecting interest, and many more—are constantly reminding investors of the potential capital growth and just how shrewd this type of investment is. But it's not them who have to live with the consequences. They have collected their reward and are making their money, regardless of whether that investment turns out to be shrewd or not. It's the investor who is left feeling confused when the strategy doesn't quite deliver on its promise.

This scenario has created an addiction to bad credit. Investors are borrowing the maximum that they can borrow, based on their income, to buy one or two investment properties. They charge the maximum rent they can get away with for the property, keep maintenance to a minimum and accept that they will have to tip in the shortfall every month to keep the monster happy. They accept this because all the vested interests have told them that it doesn't matter. The accountant reminds the investor that all their property losses are offset against their income, which could mean a nice fat tax refund. The real estate agent and the mortgage broker remind them that it doesn't matter because the property will go up in value in the next few years. All they have to do is sit tight and they can refinance the property to access the equity, therefore recouping all that the investor had to tip into the property to feed the monster. That money goes back into savings, and possibly used to buy another investment property. Any leftover is used to buy a reward for all that hard work, maybe a new car or a holiday or whatever it was the investor wanted to do that triggered the desire to invest in property in the first place.

Of course, as soon as the investor does that, they are in exactly the same position they were two or so years earlier. Their mortgage repayments have gone back up (because they have increased the loan amount by accessing the equity). But because they have not changed or upgraded the property or spent money on maintenance, they may not be able to increase the rent to help cover those costs. And so they are back to tipping more of their own money into the property in order to feed the monster, which is now $100,000 or $200,000 hungrier. It doesn't really matter that the property has gone up in value. If the investor has drawn down that equity, they have increased their debt, which will increase their mortgage payments. If they have bought another property, they are potentially even worse off in terms of cash flow, and will need to work even longer at their employed gig. Freedom? I don't think so!

But it can and does get worse. Imagine the investor now has three buy and hold investment properties. Every two or three years, they refinance to recoup the losses and gain some sense that the strategy is working (even though it's not). This is possible because the property market is still increasing. Only—what happens if it doesn't?

Before you panic, throw this book (or your ereader) against the wall, and decide to buy a lottery ticket, I believe that over the long term, property prices, barring any type of natural disaster, will go up. You don't need to be an Einstein to recognise that if the market over the long term has increased by 40 per cent but was down a few years by 3 or 4 per cent, overall it's going to be fine. But if you are an investor who is banking on the consistent linear appreciation in value so that you can cover losses, as so many Australian property investors are, then things can become unstuck really quickly.

Every property market around the world, including Australia, goes through periods of retraction or correction. Property prices may even hold steady, but without that appreciation investors can't pull out equity to cover losses, and if the contraction is significant enough it may even cause greater competition in the rental space, which means falling rental incomes. And this is especially true if the investor has been scrimping on maintenance to manage the costs.

Throw increasing interest rates into that mix and it can become downright stressful. Between May 2022 and November 2023, the Reserve Bank of Australia increased interest rates 13 times in a row.[3] It doesn't matter that interest rates were increasing from historic lows to something that was more reflective of the long-term averages. If you are an investor and interest rates are rising, your blood pressure

---

3   Hannam P (2023), 'Reserve Bank hikes cash rate by 25 basis points to 4.35%', *The Guardian*, 7 November.

is rising too. And that is the very antithesis of financial freedom. It's financial purgatory. A stagnant or depressed property market can cause real stress for those who are banking on that appreciation to recoup monthly losses and expand their portfolio.

Even when the property market is going up, other economic factors such as increasing interest and inflation rates are going to make the banks very hesitant to lend investors more money—especially if their income has not increased at the same time. This was certainly the case after the global financial crisis (GFC) in 2008, when banks the world over became much more conservative in their lending policy. More recently in Australia, the findings and recommendations from the Royal Commission into Misconduct in the Banking, Superannuation and Financial Services Industry (2017–19) meant that banks became even more conservative. The result of this tightening is that the investor simply runs out of lending road, and they are refused access to the additional funds that make the strategy at least appear valid.

This is the way that most property investors in Australia operate. They invest in long-term, buy and hold, negatively geared properties that are losing them money every month. And while they may not be happy about it, they have accepted it. Why? Because they have been told, repeatedly, that while they may lose money every month in each of their properties, one day their property will be sufficiently valuable to cover all those losses *and* create a significant nest egg for their future.

This is the system we currently have. The tax breaks can and do make property investing attractive, especially to high-income earners. But that system is only in place because the government knows that fewer people would buy property without it. If people don't buy property, governments would face a far bigger burden to house people, something they are already failing at. Governments also wouldn't be collecting as much revenue through additional property-related taxes such as capital gains tax and land tax.

The truth is it's currently almost impossible to invest in traditional buy and hold residential property and be positively geared from the start.

IS AN ALTERNATIVE STRATEGY POSSIBLE?

I've seen a significant increase in people approaching me and my company since late 2021 who have gone down the traditional property investment route. Many have created a fair amount of wealth by doing so, but it's just not working anymore. The bank has stopped lending them any more money. So these investors are carrying around their monthly losses and having to pay all the expenses, but now have no opportunity to access the built-up equity. They may have wealth on paper but they can't use it. And what's the point of having an extra million dollars on paper if you can't spend it or invest it in something else?

At this point, these investors have a dilemma. Do they stick with their assets in the hope that the market will pick up again or that the bank will reconsider, all the time having to continue to feed the hungry monster? Or do they sell one (or all) of their properties? If they sell, however, they are back in the territory of strategy one—buy and flip. Only this time, the investment has not been a new kitchen and a cosmetic face lift; it's been years and years where the investor has poured money into those assets. As soon as they sell, the value is realised and all the negative gearing benefits and tax advantages that were given by the government are recouped by the government via capital gains tax. By the time the investor pays the real estate agent selling fee, all the legal costs, the tax liability, and the outstanding mortgage (which is likely far higher than when they bought the property), they could well be facing a loss. Their best-case scenario might be that they break even, which is pretty heartbreaking considering the investment they made during the lifetime of the asset. And this is particularly likely if the investor has been extracting value along the way. All that time, effort, money and stress has come to nothing.

This is what a rock and a hard place looks like—and it feels worse. I can't tell you how many investors I've spoken to who are in this exact position. Often, they arrive at this point after years, sometimes decades, as an investor. It's soul destroying.

If one lesson emerges from the chaos for investors, it is a far greater appreciation for cash flow and the need to focus on income, not necessarily equity.

NEXT-GENERATION INVESTMENT STRATEGY

The next-generation strategy that I outline in this book still creates property that will appreciate over time, but no refinancing and pulling out of equity is required. Instead, these properties are positively geared from the start—meaning you make money on them from the start. Obviously, development costs are involved, but as soon as the buildings are complete, the development is making money. And it is highly likely to make positive monthly income forever, providing an income for you, for your children and your grandchildren.

Instead of buying a plot of land and building two townhouses on it that only a small proportion of the population can afford, this next-generation strategy is to build a rooming house with nine studio rooms on the same footprint, each with their own bathroom, kitchenette, living and sleeping space (as shown in the following figure). This is high-quality affordable housing that improves the quality of tenant's lives *and* improves returns for investors.

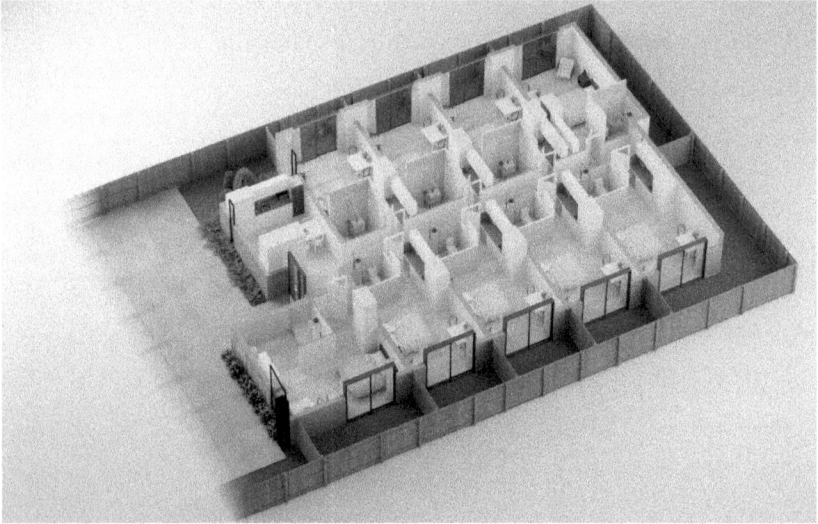

Floorplan of a nine-studio rooming house

It's worth taking a moment to rehabilitate the term 'rooming house' a little more. Rooming houses in one form or another have been around for nearly 200 years, and were particularly popular in the United States, allowing people to move to the larger cities and away from their families. In Australia, rooming houses provided affordable accommodation from around the 1850s, mostly for single men, including new immigrants and then soldiers coming back from World War I. Rooming houses continued to fill a gap in housing options and were a common accommodation choice up to the middle of the 20th century. At one point, for example, this type of accommodation housed between 5 and 10 per cent of Melbourne's population, mainly men. In the 1980s, Victoria embarked on a state-funded buy-up of grand buildings to meet a growing housing need. These properties were converted to rooming houses by various community groups.

Rooming houses have been an affordable housing option for millions around the world over many decades. They fell out of favour, however, around the 1950s and were, until recently, viewed as an accommodation choice of last resort for many on the margins of society—hence the stigma.

Since the 2000s things have been changing. While this investment type is still attractive because people still need a place to stay that will not break the bank, the appeal goes far beyond affordability.

MEETING A GROWING NEED

Importantly, this type of next-generation property investing meets a growing need for investors, tenants and society.

Investors need a better property investment strategy that doesn't turn them into wage slaves feeding endless mortgage payments and maintenance costs. They need a strategy that builds wealth not stress levels.

Rooming house investment is that strategy, allowing people to invest in property that is positively geared and that can provide ongoing income from the outset. These investors then have options— they can either enjoy that income in the here and now, or they can use that income to subsidise their negatively geared properties until the equity increases again. Either way, investors are not held to ransom by the monster, and the strategy delivers on the objective—greater financial freedom.

It's also worth pointing out that the old way of property investing often set the investor and the tenant at odds with each other. The investor was driven to screw tenants for every cent while keeping maintenance costs to a minimum. This strategy changes all that so that the investor has happy tenants who live in lovely, albeit small, homes and get on with their lives without worrying about meeting rent needs or who their weird flatmate is going to bring home next.

This win–win outcome taps into what is known as 'impact investing', where investors want to ensure that their money is doing good in the world while also delivering a return.

In 2010, JPMorgan and The Rockefeller Foundation, together with the Global Impact Investing Network (GIIN), reported that impact investment was an emerging asset class. The researchers also claimed that the asset class would reach between $400 billion and $1 trillion in assets under management by 2020. At the time, their prediction was viewed as wildly optimistic. And yet by 2020, the market had reached around $715 billion in assets under management, according to GIIN. The International Finance Corporation (IFC) put the estimate even higher at $2.1 trillion.[4]

The rise of impact investing as an asset class is demonstrating that investing doesn't have to be a zero-sum game—where there are always a few winners and lots of losers. Instead, it is possible to create win–win investments, where the investor meets a need in the marketplace that makes people's lives better *and* makes money at the same time. Baby boomers and even gen X were traditionally never that bothered about such things, but gen Y and the demographic cohort behind them, gen Z, are very interested in impact investing. They want to make the world a better place, for everyone, not just themselves.

---

4   Lamy YS, Leijonhufvud C and O'Donohoe N (2021), 'The next 10 years of impact investment', *Stanford Social Innovation Review*, 16 March.

But even if you are still more interested in return on investment, the fact remains that this strategy is meeting a growing need from tenants, which means that demand will remain high for decades to come. In Australia, we are facing a serious and growing housing crisis after decades of federal and state underfunding in social and affordable housing. A report created by UNSW City Futures Research Centre, for example, claims that 650,000 affordable or social housing homes are needed in Australia nationally over the next 15 years.[5]

The rooming house solution provides those much-needed affordable homes and makes a significant return on investment at the same time. According to the 2021 Australian Census of Population and Housing, 25.6 per cent of Australian households are lone households.[6] This figure, up from 24.4 per cent from the 2016 census, means that 1 in 4 people in Australia live alone. And yet by some estimates, only 5 per cent of all homes are one-bedroom homes.

The shortfall means that far too many people are being priced out of their area of choice. Or they are having to put up with subpar accommodation, or to share a house or even a room! New-generation rooming houses require none of those compromises, and are perfect for single people or couples.

The demand for a solution that offers people privacy and their own space without the expense, especially in our cities, is huge. And this option appeals to people across a broad age range. For the young professionals, it's not just the cost saving that is attractive, but also the time it takes to keep a studio apartment clean and tidy versus a one-

5   Troy, L, van den Nouwelant, R and Randolph, b (2019), 'Estimating need and costs of social and affordable housing delivery', City Futures Research Centre, UNSW Built Environment, UNSW Sydney.

6   Australian Bureau of Statistics (2022) 'Snapshot of Australia' https://www.abs.gov.au/statistics/people/people-and-communities/snapshot-australia/2021

or two-bedroom flat. People are busy, they don't want to be wasting their weekend tidying their apartment and they certainly don't want to be forced to eat ramen noodles five days a week in order to pay the rent. And the demand drivers are similar with the older generation who don't want the costs and maintenance associated with a larger home anymore. In addition, once a family leaves home, those who are left can often feel a sense of loneliness and social isolation that is also solved by living in these next-generation rooming houses.

I have one client who is using this strategy for older people who don't want the costs of aged care or assisted living but like the idea that if they need help or are feeling a little lonely, they can open their door and speak to their neighbour. Plus, each rooming house has a small communal area with a larger kitchen and seating area should anyone wish to use it. The tenant gets the privacy, convenience, location and affordability they want, and the investor gets a property investment strategy that delivers—rather than one that sounds good on paper but falls short.

You may have heard of the urban planning concept being pushed in Australia (and around the world) of '20-minute cities'. The idea, promoted by state governments and various NGOs, is that we need to do more to combat climate change and life more sustainably, and that we can do so by designing cities where people live within a 20-minute walk of everything they need—work, education, shopping, recreation, everything. And while the idea is great, I'm incredibly sceptical about how that can be achieved when so much of our cities has already been designed in different ways. Politicians can't, for example, tell people they can't apply for certain jobs if they are outside their radius, or that their children can't go to the school of their choosing because they live outside the radius. (And nor should they be able to!) To me, it's a nice albeit largely unworkable idea in the present situation.

Rooming houses offer a much more workable solution—and one that helps society to flourish. When more people are living in high-quality smaller spaces in their location of choice, they have a higher standard of living and more freedom too. They enjoy a shorter, less stressful commute, saving time and money. Significantly less of their disposable income is spent on housing, which means they are free to spend it in other ways that further boost local businesses and the economy. When a huge proportion of someone's salary is spent on rent, very little disposable income is left to spend in local businesses and grease the cogs of the financial system. (Remember, money is only really doing good when it is moving—either being earned or spent.) When people can find a rental solution without compromise, their levels of rental stress also diminish, which increases their physical and mental wellbeing. Happier people are also more productive, which helps more people in society to flourish.

Again, a win–win for everyone.

CHAPTER 3

REGULATIONS AND LEGALS

BEFORE I DIVE into location, site selection and how to create this type of investment, it's worth taking a step back to get really clear on what the law states around rooming houses.

These regulations and legals aren't sexy or particularly interesting, but you need to know about them. If you want to skip this chapter for now and come back to it another time, perhaps when you've decided this is the investment route for you, then do that. Just make sure you are across the legal stuff before you get going.

Each Australian state and territory has legislation relating to renting, and the rights and responsibilities of landlords and tenants. The broad definitions in these Acts are generally similar. Under Victoria's *Residential Tenancies Act 1997*, for example, a rooming house is a building where:

- one or more rooms is available for rent
- the total number of people who may occupy those rooms is four or more.

Also, in most rooming houses:

- Residents have shared access to bathrooms, kitchens, laundries and living areas.
- The owner and their family generally do not live on the premises.
- Different rental agreements are likely to exist for different residents.

Two key elements contribute to the regulation of rooming houses:

- building code
- planning requirements.

BUILDING CODE

The good news about the building code is that it is nationwide. And the Australian Building Codes Board (ABCB) sets the classifications of buildings under the National Construction Code (NCC). Two classifications are relevant to rooming houses, depending on size:

- Class 1B
- Class 3.

CLASS 1B

The Class 1B rooming house is considered a 'small' rooming house where:

- No more than 12 occupants are ordinarily resident.

- Total floor space does not exceed 300 square meters.
- The rooming house is not located above or below another dwelling or another class of building other than a private garage.

CLASS 3

If the property doesn't fit the preceding classification, it may be considered a 'shared accommodation building' which is:

- Any other building other than a building of Class 1 or 2, which is a common place of long-term or transient living for a number of unrelated people, including a rooming house, guest house, hostel or backpacker accommodation.

The difference between Class 1b and Class 3 rooming houses is important, because which classification your proposed dwelling comes under affects your obligations, such as fire safety standards and other requirements. I only build Class 1B rooming houses for reasons I'll explain shortly.

Whether you want to create a purpose-built rooming house or convert an existing building into a rooming house, the process will involve engaging with multiple local council services. You need to meet all legal requirements associated with the council's planning rules, building control and environmental health stipulations. This may include obtaining a Planning Permit, Building Permit, Occupancy Permit and registering the building as a rooming house (more on that in chapter 7).

PLANNING REQUIREMENTS

Planning relates to state government and local council regulation around what you are allowed to develop, such as how many rooms you can have in your rooming house. And, unfortunately, planning is not as straightforward as the building code because it differs wildly from state to state, and sometimes from council to council within the same state!

Queensland, for example, is council by council, whereas Victoria is unified to the whole state. In some states, recent rule changes have moved the goal posts to the point where requirements are so arduous that it becomes financially unviable. For example, in New South Wales (NSW), a change in regulation in March 2021 has effectively halted rooming house development in that state.

Advocates for affordable housing argued that the NSW laws around rooming houses allowed developers to reap government incentives for constructing rooming houses or micro-apartment developments where the rent was still too expensive for low-income earners. And while this may have been true to some extent, the cost of land in NSW is often significantly higher than in other states, which is always going to mean higher rent, even with government incentives to reduce the construction costs. But these accommodation options were still significantly cheaper than more standard one-bedroom accommodation, and offered more privacy than shared living.

However, the NSW government agreed that the old rules did not necessarily solve the problem and so changed the rules. In that state, rooming houses must be run by community providers for 10 years and rents must be set at 80 per cent of the market rate or less to ensure they are affordable. And while the changes were probably well intentioned, they have become the death knell to affordable housing in the state.[7] Existing rooming houses will carry on as before but far fewer new ones will be created. If the developer can't set the rent and ensure a profit, even a small profit, then they won't build them. That leaves government to fund them and, considering the other demands on resources, the reality is they just won't be built. Affordable housing is a gnarly problem to solve but it will only be solved with the help of private investors who can provide a much-needed service and make a return on their investment at the same time.

In Queensland, as mentioned, the rules vary from council to council, and often each council will make sure their rules are just a little bit tougher than the neighbouring council so that the applicant goes elsewhere. Quite a lot of 'NIMBY-ism' still exists when it comes to rooming houses—people may be all for affordable housing in theory, but just 'not in my back yard'. This is another reason why I want to actively call out rooming houses and rehabilitate the term, because what is being created to meet this growing need is a far cry from the image of run-down dumps full of alcoholics and drug dealers that so many people think of when they hear the term. In some councils in the Brisbane area, there is also a significant infrastructure contribution that is so high that it stops these types of developments in their tracks. Clearly, it makes sense to have some type of infrastructure contribution (to go towards the construction of community, recreation and transport infrastructure in the area) but not $100,000 per room!

People often assume that I concentrate my efforts in Victoria because I live in Melbourne, but that isn't the reason. Every state and territory government and most of the local councils are painfully aware of the need for more affordable housing, but they have sought

7   Koziol M (2021), 'Developers rush to beat the clock on affordable housing rule changes', *The Sydney Morning Herald*, 21 March.

to address that need in different ways. While they will all tell you they are creating schemes and initiatives to make it possible, only Victoria has made is straightforward. The Victorian state government has removed the red tape, made the rules very clear and then got out the way to allow private investors to build what's needed.

Essentially, the reason I focus all my efforts in Victoria is because the Victorian government has made it much easier to do business here.

I'll, therefore, focus the rest of this chapter on Victorian regulations but keep in mind that state regulations do change. It is worth keeping an eye on regulations elsewhere to see if things change in the future to follow the Victorian model. Also always double check the regulation in your state and local council at the time you are considering this investment. These things never stay the same forever.

The first piece of good news is that in Victoria a planning permit is not required if the building meets all the following requirements:

- The total floor area of all buildings on the land, measured from the outside of external walls or the centre of party walls, does not exceed 300 square metres, excluding outbuildings.
- No more than 12 persons are accommodated.
- No more than 9 bedrooms are provided.

You can build rooming houses that are larger than just specified, but they come with more regulation so I always recommend sticking to a maximum of nine studios.

The second piece of good news is that there are very clear requirements and a set of standards that must be followed and met. This means that it's very black and white—and, as an investor, I love black and white.

For example, the building regulation requirements include specifications around fire safety and access. Rooming houses must install linked smoke alarms and evacuation lighting. The installation must comply with current law and be connected to the consumer mains power where consumer power is supplied to the building.

Smoke alarms must be installed on or near the ceiling in every bedroom, and in every corridor or hallway associated with a bedroom. If there is no corridor or hallway, they must be installed in an area between the bedrooms and the remainder of the building.

A system of lighting must also be installed to assist evacuation of occupants in the event of a fire, and be activated by the smoke alarm. This must consist of a light incorporated within the smoke alarm or the lighting located in the corridor, hallway or area served by the smoke alarm.

The lighting may consist of artificial lighting that may already be installed in a corridor, hallway or area, if the lighting is activated by the smoke alarm.

In addition, the rooming house must provide access for people with a disability to at least one studio and associated sanitary facilities, as well as access to each room or space for use in common by the residents or guests, including the kitchen and laundry.

Access to the building is to be provided for all of the following:

- from the main points of a pedestrian entry at the allotment boundary
- from another accessible building connected by a pedestrian link
- from any required accessible car parking space on the allotment.

I explore these requirements in more detail in chapter 6, where I cover design and construction. For now, my point is when the rules are clear, it's very easy to build the property to comply with those rules and avoid any headaches down the track.

MINIMUM STANDARDS AND BEST PRACTISE

The Victorian government also provides a set of standards that relate to rooming house development, and if you meet those standards then local councils can't stop the development. That gives clarity, which saves time and money for both the investor and the council. There is no guesswork involved, or months lost creating an application only to have it knocked back.

Consumer Affairs Victoria provides great online resources that outline the minimum standards for rooming houses in Victoria. At the time of writing, the following minimum standards are either in force or due to become the new standard shortly. I also recommend going further than minimum standard with your development and implementing Consumer Affairs Victoria's best practise guidance.[8]

MINIMUM STANDARDS FOR EACH ROOM/STUDIO

- Any door used to enter or exit a resident's room must be fitted with a lock that is operated by a key from the outside, and can be unlocked from inside without a key.

---

8   For more information on Consumer Affairs Victoria's minimum standards for rooming houses, and to check for any changes to requirements, go to www.consumer.vic. gov.au/housing/renting/repairs-alterations-safety-and-pets/minimum-standards/rooming-house-minimum-standards.

- A key can include a device such as an electronic key fob and information used to operate a lock such as a personal identification number (PIN).
- A resident's room must have at least two power outlets in working order. These power outlets must be freely available for use by the resident and are in addition to any other power outlets already used to power amenities by the rooming house operator. The installation of any power outlets must be done by a suitably licensed or qualified electrician.
- Windows in a resident's room must have a covering that provides privacy and can be opened and closed by the resident. In addition, a window in a resident's room must be fitted with a window covering that also reasonably blocks light.

Best Practise

- The two working power outlets can be one double or two single power outlets, but not double adaptors or power boards.
- Power outlets should not be inside cupboards.
- Window coverings should be substantial enough to prevent anyone seeing into the room from the outside, including at night. Window coverings must be a kind that can be purchased by a blind supplier or those used for normal household use.

MINIMUM STANDARD FOR BATHROOMS

- A door to a shared bathroom or toilet must be fitted with a privacy latch that can be securely latched from the inside without a key. The bolt or catch must be installed by a suitably qualified person. A cabin hook or similar does not meet the minimum standard.

- If the rooming house has a shower present it must be in good working order and must have a shower head with a 3-star water efficiency rating or higher. If one cannot be installed—for example, because of the property's age—then a shower head with a 1- or 2-star rating is acceptable.

Best Practise

- A privacy latch should be strong enough to not break easily. A cabin latch does not fulfil this requirement.

MINIMUM STANDARD FOR KITCHENS

Each resident must have access to and use of food preparation facilities. These can be provided in the resident's room or as a shared kitchen.

If these facilities are in a resident's room, they must include:

- a food preparation area
- a sink
- an oven and cooktop in good working order
- a refrigerator with at least 80 litres capacity
- a cupboard with a minimum 0.1 cubic metres (100 litres) of storage capacity.

A shared kitchen must have:

- a food preparation area solely used for food preparation
- a sink

- an oven and a cooktop with four burners in good working order for every 12 or fewer residents who do not have an oven or cook-top in their room
- a refrigerator with at least 400 litres capacity
- a lockable cupboard for each resident, with a minimum 0.1 cubic metres (100 litres) of storage capacity.

Best Practise

- Bottled gas camp stoves are not suitable as they are a fire hazard.
- Cooking and preparation facilities should be located together.
- Sinks should only be provided in bedrooms if kitchenette facilities are also provided; otherwise, a sink should be in the kitchen.
- An oven provided in a bedroom must be at least large enough to hold a full-size dinner plate or medium oven dish; toaster ovens may not meet this requirement.
- Cooking facilities in bedrooms must be assessed for any fire safety risk.
- All refrigerators should have a freezer compartment.
- Lockable cupboards should be separately keyed, and each resident should have their own key.

MINIMUM STANDARD FOR DINING FACILITIES

- There must be enough chairs to accommodate the maximum number of residents that can occupy a resident's room. For example, if the room with the most occupants has three residents, the dining room must have three chairs.

- One or more tables that can comfortably fit this number of chairs must be provided. For example, a dining table can be a benchtop as long as it is large enough to accommodate the number of chairs required above, and is not a benchtop used for food preparation.

MINIMUM STANDARD FOR THE SHARED LAUNDRY

- Rooming houses must provide shared laundry facilities that are in good working order for every 12 or fewer residents.
- The laundry must include one washing machine, in good working order, for every 12 or fewer residents.
- There must be a wash trough or basin connected to a continuous and adequate supply of hot and cold water.
- There must be space with hot and cold water supply outlets suitable for a washing machine immediately next to the trough or basin.
- There must be a clothes line or other clothes drying facility.

GENERAL MINIMUM STANDARDS

- An evacuation diagram that complies with section 3.5 and Appendix E of AS 3745 must be prominently displayed in each resident's room and in all shared areas.
- Inside rooms, corridors and hallways must have a level of natural or artificial light appropriate to the function and use of the room.

- Habitable rooms must have access to natural light during daylight hours, and artificial light during non-daylight hours, appropriate to the function and use of the room.
- Habitable rooms, bathrooms, shower rooms, toilets and laundries must have ventilation that complies with the relevant Building Code of Australia (see section 18 of the Regulations).
- All gas installations, fixtures or fittings must be checked at least once every two years by a licensed gas fitter.
- All electrical installations, fixtures and fittings provided by the rooming house operator must be checked at least once every two years by a licensed electrician.
- All power outlets and electrical circuits must be connected to circuit breakers that comply with AS/NZS 3000 and switchboard-type residual current devices that comply with AS/NZS 3190, AS/NZS 61008.1 or AS/NZS 61009.1
- Each external window that can be opened must be able to be securely closed or opened without a key.
- Each external window that can be opened must also have a functioning latch, with or without a key, that secures the window against external entry.
- Each rooming house entrance must have a lock operated by a key from outside and without a key from inside. A key can include a device such as an electronic key fob and information used to operate a lock such as a personal identification number (PIN).
- The main entry must have a window, peephole or intercom system, and a working external light that provides enough light during non-daylight hours to provide for safe access and screening visitors to the rooming house.

- A rooming house must be structurally sound and weatherproof.
- A rooming house must also be free from mould and damp caused by or related to the building structure.
- Any habitable room that is likely to be used as a living area must be fitted with an internal window covering that reasonably blocks light and is one that is usually installed in a domestic household.
- All corded internal window coverings in a rooming house that have loose cords must have the cord secured to a wall by a cord guide or a cleat.

Best Practise

- Rooms should either have windows that open to allow enough air into the room, or an exhaust fan installed in the ceiling or wall, so there is adequate ventilation.
- Adequate lighting for internal rooms generally means a person should be able to comfortably read a newspaper or magazine in the room.
- Adequate lighting for corridors and hallways generally means people should be able to navigate these areas safely.
- The main entry should have enough external lighting to light the area outside the door, so residents can see who is knocking or ringing the doorbell.

GOING ABOVE AND BEYOND TO ATTRACT THE BEST TENANTS

If you are still with me and haven't fallen asleep, you will hopefully see that the rules are not arduous. They are common sense and ensure that rooming houses meet a good standard. As I mentioned, I always recommend going further, often past best practise just to ensure the best quality property.

Applying best practise or beyond in your development can bring significant benefits, including:

- improving the image and attractiveness of your property
- rehabilitating and revolutionising the perception of rooming houses in the mind of tenants
- improving the health and wellbeing of your residents, through providing a clean, safe and compact affordable accommodation solution
- increasing your profits
- setting yourself apart from the other rooming house operators who have not chosen a best practise approach.

All these benefits will of course allow you to attract and keep the best tenants who are looking for a lovely place to live that won't break the bank. In my experience, the cost of going a little further is more than recouped over the longer term.

CHAPTER 4

LOCATION AND SITE SELECTION

IN ORDER TO invest in next-generation rooming houses, you need to adopt a step-by-step approach. Whether your plan is to build the rooming house yourself or have someone else do the construction for you, you need to start with a broad look at potential locations. Then once you've found a location that ticks all your boxes, you can look for possible sites within your chosen location. (This process is shown in the following figure.)

POTENTIAL LOCATIONS

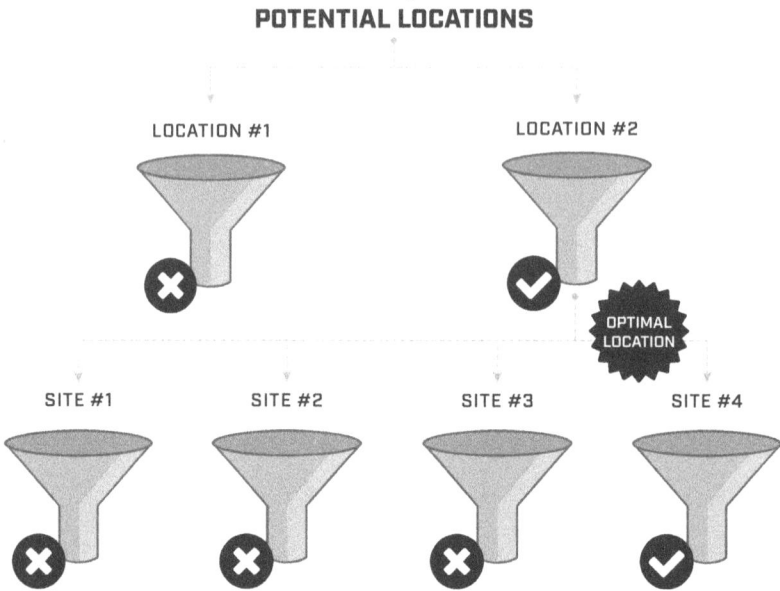

Moving from location to site selection

Let's start with finding a suitable location.

LOCATION

Like any real estate investment, location matters—however, with this strategy, the location criteria are slightly different.

When looking for the ideal location for your rooming house, you need to identify a sufficiently large area that will have more than enough potential tenants. I recommend that the town or suburb you're considering needs to have a minimum of 10,000 residents.

Once you have identified an area you are interested in, conduct some top-level research to establish whether demand for affordable housing in that area is high and not currently being met. Every rooming house in Victoria must be registered, so public data is available on existing rooming houses. (Note that different the states and territories have different regulations.) This means it is relatively easy to find out how many of these solutions have already been built in the area you are looking at.

Assuming this research looks positive, you then need to dig deeper. When you are assessing an area, you next need to answer four questions:

- Is there any abundance of prospective tenants?
- Is there a good range of services and facilities in the area?
- Are there good transport links?
- Is the site accessible?

PROSPECTIVE TENANTS

Australia is facing a nationwide shortage in good-quality, affordable housing aimed specifically at single people or couples. But it's still worth looking more deeply to identify optimal areas that will have a guaranteed stream of tenants that will want to live in the accommodation you want to create.

Does the area you are looking at have large employers or is it close to a university, for example? We have built several rooming houses close to regional hospitals in Victoria. What's particularly attractive about locations near regional hospitals as opposed to city hospitals is the availability of affordable land coupled with a steady stream of potential tenants looking for affordable accommodation. In Australia, many health professionals go on to do additional or further training in regional hospitals because placement in these positions are not as competitive as in city positions, and specialist health facilities in some of these hospitals offer advanced training opportunities. In some cases, the health professionals will then settle in that area but, more often, they will do their training and then head back to the cities where the salaries are higher. This creates a constant supply of the perfect tenant for this type of accommodation. They don't want to buy a house or pay excessive rent. Often these tenants have left their family in the city, so their singular goal is to focus on the training and visit their family when they can. All they want, therefore, is an affordable, clean and safe place to stay, in walking distance from the hospital so they can give everything to their training.

We have had a few investors, for example, build nine-studio rooming houses in proximity to a regional hospital in Victoria that is one of the biggest cancer treatment centres in the state. We managed the rentals for the first investor who built in that area and we were overwhelmed by demand—so much so that we started a waitlist. Although many doctors and nurses were completing their cancer treatment training in the hospital close by, they were not looking for long-term accommodation. The rooming house option was perfect for these tenants, and two more investors built shortly afterward in the area. This approach can also be extremely useful in predicting demand or fostering demand in a new area. Medical professionals tend to move around and what we've found is that once someone has lived in a Stone Horizon rooming house, they will often alert us about the need for a rooming house in a new location they are moving to.

Another market for potential tenants is new immigrants coming to Australia. In Australia, migrant visas are often issued with conditions that require the migrant worker to work in a regional area for a certain number of years. This is a deliberate policy to help regional economies and fill regional positions that can't be filled by the local workforce. Once the migrant worker has completed their secondment, they are free to move anywhere in Australia they want. In many cases, their jobs are again in regional health care, but it's worth looking for any large employers who are attracting this type of talent. Again, there will probably be a steady stream of good-quality potential tenants.

Another demographic to look for in your area of interest is students—although keep in mind that land close enough to a university to be attractive to students tends to be more expensive. As a result, this may be more viable in regional centres. The downside to students is they tend to be a little rowdier, and may not be as respectful of the property as other young professionals. If you opt to create a rooming house for students, you may opt for mature students or make sure all the rooms are given over to students.

We have also built rooming houses near large industrial areas with lots of blue-collar workers. Again, this is perfect accommodation for those starting out in these roles, who do not want to lose time and money on a long commute.

Industrial areas tend to behave like agricultural areas in that most people in the area work in the same industry. As an example, investors have created a couple of rooming houses in the Gippsland region in south-east Victoria. In one of them, seven out of the nine people in the property work at the same food processing plant. This wasn't a deliberate strategy but once one person moved in and loved it, they obviously went and told colleagues. Within a matter of days, the property was completely full. What's especially interesting about this property is that there is a real sense of community in the building. Because that original tenant only told people that he liked in his workplace, the group are all friends and they love living in the same space. It's affordable, they are living with their mates and it's a super easy commute to work.

SERVICES

Services are always important when it comes to location but there is a stark difference between the optimal services required for people living in a residential family home and those living in a rooming house. For example, the price of residential property tends to increase the closer it is to good schools and day care options. But good schools and day care are irrelevant for rooming houses because the tenants don't have children and often want affordable accommodation close to where they spend most of their time through the day.

Part of the attraction of this type of accommodation is that it is convenient and may be close to the tenant's place of work, but your tenants still need access to other services.

Your residents will still need access to doctors' surgeries, dentists, supermarkets, shopping centres and, ideally, some restaurants, bars and other sources of entertainment. Not all your tenants will use all the local amenities but it is always a more attractive area if those options are available to them.

TRANSPORT

Most residents of your rooming house won't have a car and will either walk or take public transport to work or to get around the area, so having these services relatively close by is always a great selling point and will help to attract the best tenants.

Again, this is not always required by all residents but having the options to jump on a bus, train or light rail a few minutes from their home is always a bonus. It really depends on who is going to occupy your property but if once you've narrowed your search and one property option has good transport links and the other doesn't, then the one with good links is the safer bet.

ACCESS

As mentioned in chapter 3, the rules around rooming house construction mean that every rooming house must have one studio that is usable by someone in a wheelchair, and all common areas must be accessible. The last consideration, therefore, is access to the prospective property. It might not make sense to choose a location that is at the top of a steep hill, for example.

It's also worth noting that the location of rooming houses are often more urban. Most people don't mind living next to a busy street if, when they go inside, the property is quiet and they can jump on a bus that stops just outside the property. Whereas a family with young children would never want to live on that road.

In addition to the strategic considerations, also consider where you want to build your rooming house, and/or who you most want to help. We have had clients who are really committed to providing solutions for older people and others who want to focus on healthcare workers as a way of saying 'thank you' while also getting a return on investment. If you have a favourite area or you would prefer to build one of these solutions in your local area, start your location search there.

SITE SELECTION

Once you've found a location that you like and you can confirm a high demand for this style of property that is currently not being met and not in the process of being met—that is, there are not half a dozen rooming houses in development—then you need to find a suitable site.

Obviously, the area you need will depend on what you plan to build. But what we've found is that the smallest rooming house that still makes financial sense by creating positive cash flow from the start is a five-studio rooming house. The minimum land size you will need for a five-studio development is around 350 square meters.

The optimal size to maximise value and return on investment is a nine-studio rooming house, and the minimum land size you would need for that is 500 square meters. It's worth pointing out that the building regulation doesn't specify that each room must have its own bathroom. It's simply that in our experience this is the optimal configuration because the bathroom adds to the rental price by increasing the value of the rooms, and gives greater privacy and independence to the tenants.

It is also possible to create larger developments of 12 or more rooms or studios in one development, but they come with additional approvals and, therefore, higher costs—which impacts viability. My recommendation, therefore, is to always stick to nine-studio developments or smaller.

Once you know what you need in terms of space, you can start to investigate your area, paying particular attention to potential sites that are close to the potential tenants that you identified in your location research. Remember, this style of living is not just attractive because it's affordable; it's in high demand because it's convenient. People just don't want to be commuting two hours a day anymore. They are simply not willing to waste so much of their time in packed trains, stuffy buses, or gridlocked traffic.

SITE SECRETS

The most important thing to remember when looking for a suitable site is that you are not building a family home. What is useable for this type of development can be very different from what is required or considered optimum for a home or even a duplex.

For example, your site doesn't need to be a perfect flat rectangular or square. A huge amount of flexibility is possible in this style of property because it can be designed to work with the site you have. For example, we have built several rooming houses on sloping sites. In one, the back of the property was 6.5 metres below the front of the property. These sites are often much less attractive and are, therefore, considerably cheaper than perfect sites. Often, they are almost 'scraps' of land that haven't been in use for 50 years or are owned by someone who has almost given up trying to sell it and is sick of paying maintenance costs on it.

In one of these sites that we ended up building on, family homes were on either side of the rooming house, but these homes had been built on the top of the site, where the builder had spent a lot of money excavating to manufacture a flat area, but the rest of the site is wasted ground. It is, of course, used as a garden but no-one is playing football in that garden any time soon. It's too steep. In both cases, the house is at the top of the plot of land, and there is a steep useless 'garden' with a shed at the bottom.

We took the same footprint and designed a nine-studio rooming house that steps down the slope. Two studios are on one level, which steps down to the next level with two more studios and so on down the slope across six different levels. The design of the rooming house meant we used all the space in the block but, more importantly, because the building was staggered down the slope, the building is not overly high, so does not look out of place in the location and doesn't block neighbours' views. We were also able to design the window placement so that everyone had a view and didn't look onto any of the neighbours.

Additional design and build costs can be associated with using less desirable land, but these costs are still usually less than buying prime real estate. It's also just a better, more sustainable use of a scarce resource, especially in areas where land is hard to come by or where ideal land is very expensive.

The flexibility that is baked into this approach allows you to take all these left over, unusually shaped areas and give them a new lease of life by turning them into functional buildings that help to alleviate the housing shortage *and* provide a return on investment. This is one of our points of difference. Whereas most investors and builders are looking for nice flat, rectangular sites, which tend to be more expensive, we have become very good at designing around sites that are not flat and rectangular so we can utilise cheaper site options while delivering a much-needed product.

In some cases, you may find a location you want to explore but then can't find any suitable sites. In which case, you will need to cycle back to the next 100 square kilometre area and start the process again. This means the process can take a while. In other instances, you might find two or three sites that have potential in your preferred location. In that situation, the best way to split them is to conduct a feasibility study on each site.

FEASIBILITY STUDY

Building a rooming house can be exciting, especially the first time. But like any other development or project, it's essential to conduct a thorough feasibility study before committing to the project. A feasibility study is a systematic analysis and assessment of the practicality, viability and potential profitability of your rooming house project. It is a way for you to minimise risk and become more familiar with any potential challenges *before* you borrow money or get too deep into the project. If the results are favourable, you can be assured upfront that the project is worth pursuing.

The main objectives of a feasibility study are to assess:

- *Technical feasibility:* This assesses whether the project can be realistically accomplished given the available technology, resources and expertise.
- *Financial feasibility:* This involves examining the project's potential costs and benefits, including initial investment in the land, construction costs, planning and operating costs, revenue projections, and potential return on investment (ROI).
- *Market feasibility:* This looks at whether there is a demand for the product or service the project aims to offer. It may involve market research, competitor analysis and identifying target demographics.
- *Operational feasibility:* This assesses whether the project can be integrated into your builder's or developer's existing operations or processes without causing significant disruptions.

- *Legal and regulatory feasibility:* This checks for any legal or regulatory constraints that the project may face, and ensures that the project complies with all relevant laws and regulations.
- *Scheduling and time feasibility:* This assesses whether the project can be completed within the desired timeframe and whether it meets any critical deadlines.

Rigorous feasibility analysis allows you to determine whether the site you have found is workable or you need to modify the plans or abandon them altogether and look for a better site. Feasibility studies play a crucial role in risk assessment and can save you a huge amount of time and resources by avoiding ill-conceived projects that will not deliver the desired outcome.

The financial feasibility is the most important aspect to consider, and I've included a video of me outlining how to conduct a financial feasibility in the resources section of the website dedicated to this book—just go to roominghousemillionaire.com/resources.

CHAPTER 5

SECURING FINANCE

IN THIS CHAPTER, I unpack the options for securing finance for rooming house developments. But before I do so, let's step back a moment to consider what type of rooming house you want to create.

CONVERSION OR NEW BUILD?

A lot of misconceptions exist about whether it is better to convert an existing property to a rooming house or to design and build something from scratch. All too often, which approach is considered best depends on who you are talking to and their vested interests rather than what's best for you as an investor. In my business, we help clients to create both and the final choice depends on the client and their needs, not what we would prefer to build. I cycle back to the difference between conversions and purpose-built rooming houses in the next chapter (where I discuss design and construction), but I'm introducing the concepts here because your choice influences the types of finance that will be available to you.

The conversions strategy is to buy an existing house and reconfigure, change and add to the internal layout to create several separate studios with some common areas. An older style large family home, for example, may have multiple bedrooms, multiple living areas, as well as a dining room or rumpus room that may not have been used that much when the property was a family home. All those rooms might be able to be converted into separate studios with a kitchenette and ensuite. Or the internal layout can be redesigned to create those separate spaces, potentially with some additional rooms added on.

When most people first hear about investing in rooming houses, this type of conversion is what springs to mind. And this is exactly what I did myself. I bought a house and then converted that property to a rooming house using money from my own savings.

But a rooming house is not just a house with lots of individually rented rooms; there are a whole bunch of additional requirements that most people don't think about, particularly around compliance, fire safety and access (more on those in the next chapter).

Converting an existing building is also not the only way to create a rooming house. The alternative is a purpose-built rooming house, where you design the property from the ground up. Instead of trying to find ways to make an existing house work for this new purpose, the purpose-built design optimises the space from the start to create the best possible outcome for the investor and the tenant.

As mentioned, your choice also influences your funding options.

FUNDING OPTIONS

You can fund your rooming house investment in six main ways:

1. cash
2. residential finance
3. commercial finance
4. private lending
5. joint venture
6. hybrid.

The following table provides a quick snapshot on what finance is possible when you're considering a conversion, versus a purpose-built five- or nine-studio rooming house.

	Conversion	Five-studio rooming house	Nine-studio rooming house
Cash	✔	✔	✔
Residential finance	✔	✔	✘
Commercial finance	❔	❔	✔
Private lending	✔	✔	✔
Joint venture	✔	✔	✔
Hybrid	✔	✔	✔

Funding options for rooming house development type

CASH

The easiest or most straightforward option is to use cash to finance the development of a rooming house, and that is true regardless of whether you want to convert an existing property or build a purpose-built rooming house. The cash may come from savings or you may be able to use money currently tucked away in superannuation—although you would need to check the rules of your fund. You may also be able to access cash by releasing equity in other assets.

The advantage of cash is that you already have it and don't have to worry about application forms and interest rates. Obviously, by using your own cash you don't have ongoing debt servicing costs eating into your return, and your cash flow will increase over time. But most people don't have enough cash to fund the whole development.

If an investor does have access to cash, what we regularly see is that the investor will use their cash to either buy the block of land or the property they plan to convert. This allows them to minimise costs while the planning and paperwork is being finalised. They will then secure funding for the construction phase.

For those who don't have access to large chunks of cash, however, many other funding options are available.

RESIDENTIAL FINANCE

The existing perception is that financing a conversion is easier than a purpose-built rooming house, and to some extent it is. Most people have gone through the process of buying their own home and securing a mortgage for this property, so they are familiar with residential finance. It can feel safer and less risky—even though it's neither.

This type of finance does have some advantages beyond perceived simplicity and comfort, however. The first is the interest rate. The mortgage rates on residential loans are always lower than those on commercial loans. Plus, you may be entitled to even lower interest rates if you belong to a particular profession. In Australia, for example, most of the major banks classify a certain group of professions as 'lower risk', which entitles eligible borrowers to special interest rate discounts. Those professions include medical professionals, those in some professional services, entertainment professionals and, bizarrely, sports professionals. I'm not sure how an AFL player is considered low risk but those are the rules!

The second big advantage is the loan-to-value ratio (LVR). The LVR is a financial metric that expresses the ratio of a loan amount to the appraised value or purchase price of a property. It is typically expressed as a percentage.

The LVR helps lenders assess the level of risk associated with a mortgage loan. A higher LVR indicates that the borrower is taking out a larger portion of the property's value as a loan, which can increase the lender's risk if the property's value was to decrease.

For example, say you're purchasing a property that has an appraised value of $1,000,000. If you're applying for a mortgage with a loan amount of $800,000, the LVR would be calculated as follows:

- LVR = (Loan amount ÷ property value) × 100
- LVR = ($800,000 ÷ $1,000,000) × 100
- LVR = 80%

In this case, the LVR is 80 per cent, meaning you are borrowing 80 per cent of the property's value and contributing a 20 per cent deposit.

Lenders often have LVR limits, meaning they may have maximum allowable ratios for different types of loans. And these rules are always more favourable for residential finance, which means you may be able to borrow 90 per cent or 95 per cent of the value of the property, lowering the amount of your own money you need to use. (Keep in mind you may also have to pay mortgage insurance with this higher LVR.)

The lower interest rates on offer—and especially if you can tap into the discounts on offer for lower risk professions—together with accessing a more favourable LVR makes residential finance a good option.

However, residential finance does come with more rules. Importantly, one of the limitations of this type of finance is that it is only possible to use residential finance when you plan to build a smaller rooming house of five rooms (or fewer) or plan to buy a property to convert.

Banks want to know that if things go wrong, they can repossess the house and sell it on the residential market. This is tricky for a nine-studio rooming house but is more than feasible for a five-room rooming house. The new owner would just need to convert one of the bedrooms into a living room and all the bedrooms have their own bathroom—something that is increasing common in residential housing anyway.

If you were buying a property to convert it, residential finance would also be an option. The loan would only secure the property, however. You would still need money to pay for the conversion.

The average conversion costs about $100,000—money that the bank that gave you the residential mortgage will not finance. In fact, even asking them to fund the conversion will likely spook them and they may very well change the terms of your finance. If you plan to convert a large family home to a seven-studio rooming house, for example, the bank is likely to suggest that is no longer in the scope of residential finance. Again, residential lending is for houses or properties that can be easily converted to a house for a 'regular' family to live in. A rooming house doesn't fit that definition so most banks just won't lend residential finance if they know you plan to convert the property into a rooming house with more than five studios. And if they find out after you've bought the property, they may change the loan to a commercial loan anyway!

This means that you will have to find the $100,000 from your own savings, like I did, or get the additional money from somewhere else.

The other significant drawback to residential finance is that you need to prove that you have enough income from other sources to cover the repayments. You need to prove that you can service the loan from income other than the potential rental income. This means that even if you do decide to use residential finance to pay for rooming house conversions, you will eventually hit a borrower ceiling where the bank just refuses to give you any more money because you can't cover all the repayments from other income. And, more importantly, they won't allow you to refinance so you can't get access to any growth in value.

Again, this happened to me and I hadn't anticipated it. That first rooming house I created will probably never be refinanced. As I said, banks get a little funny about you changing the use of the property. If you buy a large house with the intention of converting that into a rooming house, the bank may object because in their eyes you are potentially decreasing the value of their asset. Of course, you are not decreasing the value of the asset but banks tend to like borrowers to stick within tight guidelines and rules, and anything a little different or unusual, such as a rooming house, is likely to run into problems with the lender, certainly a residential lender. Those making lending decisions basically have a tick box list of what's acceptable, and changing the use of the house is not always considered acceptable. As a result, refinancing becomes next to impossible. If I were to go back to the bank that gave me the mortgage initially, they would send someone out to revalue it and that person would hit the panic button. To them they lent me money to buy a house, and they expect that the house to still be a traditional house, and probably won't even have the experience to value it properly. I can't pull equity from the property and even if I tried to refinance with another lender the process would alert the loan manager, who might start asking awkward questions and could reclass the asset and change the loan conditions. The reality, therefore, is if you do decide to pursue this strategy and access residential finance, you will probably have to fund the conversion yourself or get a separate commercial loan from another lender. And you will not have easy options to refinance.

What is important to note is that once you factor in all the costs, the overall cost of a conversion is not that much different to the cost of a purpose-built property. And as I will explain in the next chapter, the advantages of a purpose-built rooming house far outweigh any minimal saving you may make on interest payments.

In my experience, both personally and with my clients, a conversion makes the most sense financially when an investor already owns a suitable house as part of their existing property portfolio. Perhaps that property is not performing as a typical rental but could be turned into a cash cow as a rooming house. This strategy can become even more potent if the value of the property is significantly higher than the existing mortgage on the property. This would allow the owner to refinance to gain access to the money that will be needed for the conversion. In this scenario, using residential finance to convert an existing house to a rooming house is a shrewd choice. Instead of waiting for capital appreciation, you are converting that property to a high-yield cash flow property. This is the main reason we still do conversions today at my business. We have many clients who owned a suitable property but it wasn't performing, so converting that property to a positive cash flow property made sense. Instead of getting one rent, they are now getting five or even seven rental payments per week for the same property. It also sometimes makes sense if for whatever reason the configuration of rooms in the house is already very well set up for a rooming house conversion, so the costs may be considerably lower than the average $100,000.

COMMERCIAL FINANCE

For those who don't have ready cash or their development will not easily quality for residential finance, commercial lending is a great option. This is the funding that I use most of the time.

Rooming houses are a specialised asset designed to provide affordable accommodation for tenants and produce cash flow for investors. As such, they are considered by many lenders as commercial assets. Even though the asset is technically a residential asset because people are going to live in that property, it behaves more like a commercial asset. But this isn't necessarily a bad thing, especially if you can find yourself an experienced and capable broker.

Commercial finance certainly has pros and cons. Let's get the disadvantages out the way first. The main one is that the interest rates on offer for commercial finance are almost always higher than those for residential finance. This is because this asset class is perceived as higher risk. But interest rate is not the only determinant on whether a final solution is good or not.

The reason I use commercial finance more than any other type is because your ability to access residential finance depends on your ability to prove that your other income can comfortably service the loan. But this is not the case with commercial finance. To be accepted for commercial finance, all you need to do is prove that the income from the asset you are creating will service the loan. Banks and finance providers are, therefore, less interested in your personal financial position. And because rooming houses are one of the few asset classes in this country where the rental income should easily cover the loan—and leave some money left over—it's often easier to get over the line.

This is critically important for a certain set of investors. I have several clients, for example, who have decided to either use their super or otherwise access other money to invest in rooming houses. But once they have retired and no longer have an income, getting a traditional residential mortgage is almost impossible because suitability assessment relies on whether the borrower can service that debt from other income. The commercial finance option bypasses those issues.

The second reason I love commercial finance is valuation potential. Commercial properties, including rooming houses, mostly get valued based on the income they generate. This means that the value of the property increases as the income generated by that property increases. This does a couple of incredibly good things. The first is that when you finish the rooming house and rent the studios to tenants, the valuation based on that collective rental income is usually significantly higher than the total costs of creating that property. And this valuation only goes up.

You no doubt know about, and may have experienced, the cycles, peaks and troughs of residential real estate. A whole bunch of things, which you have no control over, can impact the value of your house. However, those aspects don't usually impact the value of commercial real estate because that value is linked to income—not outside factors that can influence demand for residential property, such as the economy or changes to political policy.

I've personally seen my own home increase and decrease in value over many years; it is always cyclical. But what I've never seen is rents go down. The value of residential property may fluctuate, but rents don't. If I were to plot a line of rental income across my rooming houses from the point they were finished onwards, rents have always gone up. I'm still offering affordable solutions because the rent in a rooming house is always affordable in relation to alternatives in the area. When those alternatives go up so does the rent in rooming houses. And this increase in value allows you to access that value to build another rooming house or use that value in a different way.

For me, commercial finance is the best solution because of its flexibility and valuation capabilities. It may have slightly higher interest rates but the benefits easily compensate for this factor.

PRIVATE LENDING

The next funding option open to you is private lending. As the name suggests, private lending is where you borrow the money you need from a private source. This may be from a 'family office' (a private wealth management advisory firm that serves ultra-high-net-worth individuals) or directly from a high-net-worth individual who is looking to invest their money for a good return.

The biggest advantage of this type of finance is you usually have a lot of flexibility while getting to keep most of the return. Private lending doesn't really abide by the same rules as institutional lending, either residential or commercial.

The terms tend to depend on the individual or entity you are dealing with and the business case you have put forward, but this type of lending is always over a far shorter time frame than traditional bank lending. This is ideal for the private lender who doesn't want to get locked into long positions, and it's ideal for you because you get the money you need to get the rooming house up and running. The interest rates are always high for private lending, but it can still make sense over the short term and is often easier and more flexible to arrange.

As soon as the construction is finished, simply re-finance the rooming house on better terms elsewhere. The private investor is happy because they have their money back together with a nice return and they repeat the process elsewhere. You are happy because you have your asset and have refinanced at a better rate.

This is a good option for getting the costs for construction met. The biggest challenge with private lending is access. These lenders do not deal with retail and are usually only accessible via a reputable broker. It took me many years of trial and error to find a network of reputable, experiences brokers who can now connect investors to this funding source.

JOINT VENTURE

Joint venture (JV) is another funding option that has huge potential. It is essentially when a few or a group of people come together to create the rooming house. Obviously, this can be very useful if individual investors don't have access to all the money they need. That said, this option is fraught with potential risks. My advice on this approach is to only pursue it with people you know very well, such as childhood friends or family members. But that is still no guarantee of success.

Regardless of who you enter a joint venture partnership with, you need to have a written and signed agreement between all parties that sets out the parameters of the agreement and covers what will happen if one of the partners needs to exit the agreement. The idea is to consider all the things that could go wrong, and have a process in place for handling those things, *before* they occur.

If you can get those potential future issues ironed out and agreed on, this can be a brilliant way to invest in rooming houses.

I remember one investor who absolutely loved this strategy and was super excited to build a nine-studio rooming house but he didn't have the money, so he approached his parents and they created a JV agreement. They went on to build the rooming house, sharing the rental income.

Just make sure you get everything in writing. A good JV agreement should include:

- *Parties to the agreement:* The agreement begins by identifying and naming the parties entering the joint venture, including their legal names, addresses and any other relevant contact information.
- *Purpose and objectives:* This should be a clear statement outlining the purpose and objectives of the joint venture. This section defines what the parties aim to achieve through their collaboration.

- *Contributions and obligations:* This details the contributions each party will make to the joint venture, which will include financial investments, assets or expertise. The agreement should also outline the responsibilities and obligations of each party.
- *Management and decision-making:* This section specifies how the joint venture will be managed, including the appointment of key personnel, decision-making processes and voting rights.
- *Capital structure:* This describes the financial structure of the joint venture, including capital contributions, profit-sharing arrangements and any additional financing requirements.
- *Distribution of profits and losses:* This defines how profits and losses will be allocated among the joint venture partners. This section can be quite detailed and should address various scenarios.
- *Governance and control:* This section addresses issues related to governance, including the appointment of key executives, voting rights and the role of each partner in decision-making.
- *Term and termination:* This specifies the duration of the joint venture and the circumstances under which it can be terminated or extended. It may also cover exit strategies and buyout provisions.
- *Dispute resolution:* This outlines the process for resolving disputes between the joint venture partners, which may involve mediation, arbitration or other mechanisms.
- *Reporting and accounting:* This section sets forth the financial reporting and accounting procedures, including how financial records will be maintained, audited and distributed among the parties.

- *Insurance and liability:* This addresses issues related to liability, insurance coverage and indemnification in case of legal claims or losses.
- *Exit strategies:* This contains provisions for what happens if a partner wants to exit the joint venture, including the sale of their interest or the buyout process.
- *Miscellaneous clauses:* In addition to the factors just listed, the JV agreement will have other clauses, such as governing law, dispute resolution and any other special provisions tailored to the specific needs of the joint venture.

If you embark on a JV, be sure to get legal advice to help draft the legal agreements to ensure that the terms and conditions align with the parties' intentions and that all legal requirements are met. Money does odd things to people, even family members and long-term friends, so just get all the bases covered and to help avoid any hassle down the track.

HYBRID FINANCE

Hybrid finance is the last option and is essentially just a mix of some of the earlier methods.

For example, if you decide to buy a large house and convert that into a rooming house, you may buy the property using residential finance to tap into the lower interest rates and then secure separate commercial finance from a different institution to pay for the conversion.

A common scenario with some of my investors is to use cash to secure the land to build the property. This means they have no debt servicing costs as the designs and permits are finalised. They then secure private funding for a short burst of six to nine months to pay for the construction. This is always at a high interest rate, but it works because it's super flexible. Then when the property is finished and the studios rented out, it's valued based on this rental income and re-financed into a longer term commercial loan with far lower interest rates.

It's all about getting the best mix of finance for you and your project.

Finance is just a tool that you will need to realise your ambitions. All the solutions covered in this chapter are valid, and which one is best for you will depend on whether you are building a rooming house from scratch or converting an existing building, as well as your own stage of life and personal circumstances. No solution is better or worse, some are just easier to arrange and cheaper than others but the priority is securing the finance. Plus, you need to remember that once the asset is created, you will have far more options, should you want to explore them to re-finance and secure better terms.

CHAPTER 6

DESIGN AND CONSTRUCTION

ONCE YOU HAVE your finance in place (as covered in the previous chapter), the next step is design and construction. This is the juicy bit. Of course, the design of the rooming house will depend on whether you are redesigning an existing property or building the rooming house from scratch, so let's dive into that first.

CONVERSION VERSUS PURPOSE-BUILT ROOMING HOUSES

It's worth cycling back to this discussion one last time because it impacts design and construction. Converting an existing property and creating a purpose-build rooming house both have merit. What is going to be best for you and your investment portfolio will depend on your existing resources and whether you have a property that is ripe for conversion in your portfolio already. But if you are going to have to buy the property to convert into a rooming house, as I mention in the previous chapter, there is often not that much difference in cost.

I believe that purpose-built rooming houses provide not only a much higher quality product for the tenants but also ultimately a much better return for the investor. Win–win. Putting finance options aside, additional reasons make purpose-built rooming houses better, and you need to be aware of these upfront.

The first difference is the quality of the finished product. I'm not talking about the quality of the construction or the finish, but the perception of the accommodation by the tenants. When you convert an existing house into a rooming house, you inevitably inherit the existing layout of the house. And because of that you are always limited or restricted on what sort of changes and design you can implement in each individual room or studio. And unless you are incredibly lucky and have a layout or floorplan that is perfect to create separate accommodation, you are going to have to make some compromises. And your tenants are going to have to live with those compromises—which colours their experience of your rooming house. Those compromises are far less likely to occur when you design the rooming house from scratch with the purpose of making the experience of all tenants the best it can be.

And quality does matter. Ensuring the best possible quality for your budget so that you maximise the tenant experience translates into rental value. The feeling and vibe we're able to achieve in Stone Horizon rooming houses is very similar to the feeling someone would get from living in a studio apartment. They are like apartments I've seen in New York City, for example. When you design from scratch, you can build in a sense of independence and privacy that is very hard to create in a conversion, just because of the nature of the original building. This independence and privacy is highly valued by tenants, meaning this type of purpose-built property is often far easier to rent and, subsequently, the rent paid is higher. When you have more demand for the type of property you've create, you as the owner have more choice as to who you accept as tenants and what level the rent is set at.

And this is not just a guess. I've looked at this statistically and tracked rental income across all sorts of property types, accounted for location and other factors, and found purpose-built rooming house can make up to $500 a week more than conversions. That's a significant amount of money over the long term. Again, this is not about gouging your renters. You're still offering an affordable option, but can set the rent that little bit higher because of the higher quality.

The second reason quality is important is because it influences the type of tenant who will want to live in the rooming house. This was something that I knew intuitively but it was only once my business started to build purpose-built rooming houses that it was proven. Again, we looked at the applications that were being made for other properties in the area—including other studios, shared housing, converted rooming houses and our purpose-built option—and found the calibre of tenant to the purpose-built rooming house was significantly higher. Unsurprisingly, the best properties get the best tenants and that is true regardless of what is happening in the rental market. This is massively important because it means that most of our tenants are employed professionals or those in later life looking to downsize. They want to live somewhere that is clean, functional and easy to maintain, and they tend to look after their property as though it were their own.

The last reason that quality is important is the tenants stay longer. This was actually a huge surprise to me. But, again, I looked at the data across all properties managed by my business. Not only did our investors earn more money from good quality purpose-built rooming houses than from conversions, but they also attracted a better quality of tenant and those tenants stayed longer.

My recommendation to investors is that if they have an existing building in their portfolio and want to try the rooming house strategy in that property first, do it. But if they don't have a house in their portfolio already, then the purpose-built option is almost always the best approach. I and my team also conduct thorough discovery calls with investors to really dig into their situation to see what is best for them and their short- and long-term goals.

The remainder of this chapter, however, focuses on design and construction of a purpose-built rooming house.

PURPOSE-BUILT DESIGN

The design of your property will obviously depend on the footprint of the area you've acquired. For example, towards the end of chapter 4 I talk about a rooming house we built on a steep slope. Instead of excavating to level off the site, we used the slope and staggered studios down it to create a better product so that each studio had a view. Although it was a more complex build, the increased build cost was offset by the reduced cost of the land and the result was better for the tenants.

It's also incredibly important to design your rooming house so that it is in keeping with the other properties in the area. When I first started Stone Horizon to build this type of property for myself and others, we would keep signage to a minimum and purposefully pursue a low-key construction strategy. But it never really worked. People in the area would always find out that we were building a rooming house and our low-key approach ended up creating more trouble than it was worth. We now put up signage right from the early stages and engage with the neighbours any chance we get, so that they can be reassured that not only what is being build is in keeping with the other properties in the area but also the tenants will not be drug dealers and criminals.

Rooming houses still get people worried. That's just a fact, at least for the time being. My hope is that over time, people will recognise that a rooming house is not just a brilliant investment for those looking to create financial freedom but also a way to provide a much-needed and much-loved affordable housing solution for people of all ages. As I've mentioned, most of our rooming houses are let to either young professionals or those in the later stages of life who don't want the hassle and cost of a large family home (and I provide more on possible residents in chapter 8). The sooner everyone realises just how good rooming houses are for society, tenants and investors, the better.

In many of the properties we create, some people in the area don't even realise it's a rooming house because it looks exactly like the rest of the properties on the street or in the area. This is very deliberate—not to hide the purpose of the property but to ensure the building itself blends in to its surrounding. For example, one property we built in Gippsland looks exactly like the other four-bedroom homes in the area—at least from the outside. On the inside, of course, the property did not have a dining room or a rumpus room, and the space was maximised to create nine separate studios and some shared spaces. In another example, we were building the rooming house in a 'smarter' part of town and the investor wanted it to blend into that area, so we chose a more architectural look and feel for the building.

Whatever the outside of the building looks like, the design is always using the footprint of the land most efficiently and in a way that fits into its surroundings. We also make sure that maintenance requirements are super low. For example, we never include a front or shared garden—that's just wasted space and no-one wants to mow the lawn. Instead, we landscape the area around the building with a few hardy succulents that will grow without any interference or we just have some mulch and landscaping pebbles. That way, neither the tenants nor the investor has to worry about maintaining the shared outside spaces of the property. Instead, the investor or managing agent just needs to remove any weeds peeking through the gravel or paving every month or so. Job done. (Tenants often have small private outdoor spaces that they can decorate or add potted plants to as they like.)

STUDIO DESIGN

As mentioned in the introduction, in some places in the world people are very used to small spaces. And the most innovative and funky are probably in New York and Tokyo. I always spend time in these places to get more inspiration and see what's possible. I've also lost count of the YouTube videos that people have sent me of tiny spaces with drop-down beds and moving walls that transform a space—for example, a living area into a home office. Some are a bit naff and clunky but others are super slick and very cool.

And it's certainly easy to see the marketing and resident appeal to these types of dynamic spaces. But no-one talks about the downside of drop-down beds and moving walls, especially over the long term. Many years ago, I used to work for the car manufacturer Toyota. And one of the first things that was drummed into us was that moving parts are bad. Moving parts wear out. Moving parts break. In cars, it's the moving parts that cause problems and send you to the mechanic. And the same is true for just about everything in life, including our homes.

Those tiny spaces may look funky in marketing videos but what happens then you press the button and the bed doesn't drop down over the couch or, worse, gets stuck halfway down so you can't use the bed or the couch? What happens when the wall won't move back to give you a living space again? If there are moving parts—and these types of properties have a lot of moving parts—they will break down. It's inevitable. As a result, you as the investor will face a lot of extra expense because contractors need to access those moving parts, which are usually hidden away behind walls. And it's an inconvenience and disruption for your tenant.

These types of dynamic spaces may look great but they are often not practical. They are expensive to install and they will require more investment to maintain. But, perhaps even more importantly, they won't even get used. People are set in their ways and they will usually opt for the course of least resistance. Let me give you an example here. In the early days, we used to install a flip-up table that was attached to the wall. The tenant could use the table when they needed to and put it down so it was flat against the wall when they didn't need it. Only what we found was that they either left it up or never used it at all. They certainly didn't use it as intended. And the same often holds true for these funky studios with moving walls. The tenant will move in and the novelty of the design will captivate them for a week. The bed will be dropped down at night and put back up in the morning and the study will be used every night. But give that tenant a week or two and the bed is down all the time. The moveable wall to create the study hasn't been touched and instead they are studying on their laptop while sitting on the bed watching TV.

That's just the nature of human beings, especially at home where we want to relax. Very few people want to be assembling tables every time they need them—and no-one wants to be dropping down the bed as they stumble in after a big night out!

I and my team have asked our tenants and they don't live in the studios because the studios belong on the cover of *Vanity Fair*. They love the studios because they are functional and have everything they need without them needing to sacrifice their life to pay for a massive rent or mortgage—or needing to sacrifice their time cleaning a larger home that they don't really use.

Today, we design with two things in mind:

1. functionality
2. durability.

We don't waste time with flip-up tables because our tenants don't want them. They want a sturdy table with a couple of chairs and they want a bed that is only a bed. Historically, I've seen so many investors make big mistakes with design where aesthetics takes priority over durability and functionality and no-one wins.

Your investment and your tenants' experience are far better served by having the least amount of moving parts as possible in your development *and* by setting up the studios as they will be used with functional, durable furniture that was designed for one job. No-one wants the hassle of pressing buttons or manually moving walls along runners. It sounds simple and easy but the reality is that most people will find a configuration that works for them most of the time and leave it at that. Our philosophy is to provide that configuration from the start.

It's also essential that you see these studios through the eyes of the tenant, not your own. You're not designing the studios based on what you might want to live in. For generations, in Australia and around the world, our home was viewed as our castle. We would live and socialise in the house, whether that was dinner with the family or weekend BBQs with friends. Our home was the place we spent most of our free time. But that isn't how potential tenants see these studios. A growing demographic, and it's not just young professionals, don't see where they live as the place they spend most of their free time. Instead, their home is simply their base. They leave to go to work, might come home and change, and then go out again to meet friends. Instead of the backyard BBQ, they will meet their friends at the beach and use the open-air BBQ facilities. Or they will go out to dinner or off to the gym. Their home is where they sleep and relax before going out to meet friends and family. The only difference between your potential tenants and the rest of the renting population is they have realised it makes no sense to spend so much of their income on rent when they only really sleep in the property.

How many people have skimped and saved for the bigger house with the second living room or extra bedroom that no-one ever sets foot in? Many people, especially single people and couples without children, are realised they have far more interesting things to spend their money on. It's going to be incredibly important moving forward as you help find solutions to the variety of housing needs that you, as an investor, don't project your own concept of ideal housing or your own history or experience of property onto the new generation of tenants or investors. I still live in a lovely large family home because

I have a young family and we enjoy the space and spending time together but, beyond my own home, the only type of investment property I own are rooming houses that meet the needs of people at a different stage in their lives.

FURNISHING

Over the years at my business, we have experimented with a lot of designs and layouts in the rooming houses we've built. We've worked out that the optimal configuration is almost always a nine-studio, purpose-built rooming house that is rented furnished.

Furnished studios are ideal for most of the tenants we want to attract because they often arrive with a suitcase. A student or a young professional who has just moved out of home for the first time (or just arrived in the country) doesn't want to trek off to the nearest IKEA or Harvey Norman and spend thousands on basics such as a bed, table and chairs. And they certainly don't want to have to put all that stuff up for sale again when they move out. Moving in to a new place where all the essentials are already provided is far more convenient and attractive to most of our tenants.

Most tenants also expect to pay slightly higher rent for that convenience, which adds to the revenue. A good, functional and durable furniture package for each of the nine studios might cost about $30,000, which usually works out to be around 2 to 3 per cent of the total cost of the development (including land and construction costs). However, you can add 10 per cent to the rent for that convenience, and continue to do so year after year. (You will, of course, have some continued replacement costs as items wear out.)

Providing a furniture package is a good deal for the tenant and it's a good deal for you. In our properties we provide:

- a double bed (with mattress and mattress protector)
- a small table and two chairs
- a fridge
- microwave oven
- kettle
- toaster.

The other reason we furnish each studio is because we don't want people lugging too much of their own stuff into the property. If a studio becomes too cluttered, it can become a fire hazard. Plus, we're less likely to have to fix damage to walls that can so easily happen when moving large items of furniture such as a bed. The main items they need are already provided. They can unpack, and get on with their life. Conversely, when it's time to leave they can pack up, clean the studio and hand in the keys. No hassle.

CONSTRUCTION

Three key things make construction of a purpose-built rooming house different from a normal family home:

1. insulation
2. fire safety
3. universal access.

INSULATION

Normally when a residential house gets built, the external walls of the property are insulated for thermal efficiency. This ensures the residents are comfortable all year around and that the heat doesn't come in during the summer or escape during the winter. In a purpose-built rooming house, every single wall in between the studios or in between the studios and common areas must also be insulated. This is done for a couple of reasons. The first is to provide sound insulation so that a person in one studio is much less likely to hear the person in the next studio. This is a legal requirement of rooming house construction.

By having this type of insulation in your rooming house, you improve the peace and quiet inside each studio so your tenants feel more like they have neighbours rather than house mates. Each studio has a sense of isolation and privacy from the other studios and from the common areas.

The second reason to install this insulation is thermal efficiency. This helps when two different tenants want to have their heating or cooling at different temperatures. The insulation prevents the two systems from constantly fighting each other, which saves energy and reduces your utility costs.

Insulation is measured using what is known as the 'R-value'. The higher the R-value, the better the insulating property of the material. We use R2.5 between internal walls. (The minimum required for standard wall insulation in Victoria in R1.5.) You can achieve this level of insulation in a couple of ways.

One option is to use normal thermal insulation, like the insulation used in the external walls. Although it is called thermal insulation, its key advantage for the internal walls in rooming houses is the sound insulation, but it has several additional advantages. It is easy to install, easy to remove if it ever needs to be replaced or repaired, and it very affordable.

The other option is a type of insulation called Soundcheck. This is the same type of insulation that is used between apartments. By putting this thick plaster in between the two frames in the internal walls, you not only get great sound insulation between studios but also provide a degree of fire protection. There is very little difference between the two options in terms of thermal capacity, but you have the added benefit of additional fire safety with the Soundcheck option.

FIRE SAFETY

Fire safety is the second construction difference between rooming houses and a normal family home.

In a traditional house, the level of mandatory fire protection is limited. You may need to have working smoke detectors in the living and sleeping areas, for example, but they don't need to be linked. The assumption is that in a traditional house or even in a shared house where a family or group of people are living together, if something goes wrong the residents would alert each other of the danger and get out the house. But in a rooming house, that assumption doesn't stand. It probably would be true that if something happened, residents would knock on their neighbour's door and alert them to danger but this can't be assumed. In a purpose-built rooming house, all the smoke detectors in the property must be linked and hardwired so that if one goes off, they all go off.

Ensuring this is important, and not just to comply with regulation. There is a greater risk of fire in a rooming house than in a traditional house. In a traditional home, most fires start in the kitchen. And a nine-studio rooming house has ten kitchens! This includes the main one in the shared space and nine kitchenettes in each studio, each with a toaster, kettle and potentially a microwave. Linking the smoke alarms in this way makes the rooming house safer and potentially limits the damage caused should a fire breakout.

To ensure that anyone can react to a fire should it occur, each rooming house must also have fire extinguishers in the common areas, usually the kitchen. Legally these need to be checked every six months and recertified every year. This is part of the compliance and insurance conditions that are required to maintain a rooming house registration and licence (more on that in chapter 7).

The next fire safety condition is emergency lighting and exit signs. You may have noticed a theme by now in that rooming house regulation lives somewhere between a residential property and a commercial property. And the emergency lighting and exit sign requirements certainly tilt toward commercial.

You are required to provide an external light and a special type of artificial lighting, like you see in commercial buildings or apartment buildings. This lighting comes on if the main lighting goes out and directs residents to the exit—if their vision is impaired by smoke, for example. And each rooming house must display the kind of large, easily seen exit signs that are common in hotels or offices.

Whether it is really needed in a five- or nine-studio rooming house is up for debate but the regulation states that each rooming house must have an exit sign and the little green running man to tell everyone how to get out. And if it's part of the regulation, you need to comply.

UNIVERSAL ACCESS

Also known as disability access, universal access simply means that when you build your rooming house you must provide a room, bathroom and basic common facilities that are accessible by someone in a wheelchair. That is the law, but these spaces don't need to be used by someone in a wheelchair. It's perfectly acceptable to rent the wheelchair accessible studio to anyone; it doesn't need to be rented to someone with a disability. Same with the accessible toilet and common areas—the law says they must be provided but makes no stipulation as to who can use them.

To be clear about the common areas, these regulations mean that the main kitchen in the common area of the property and the laundry need to be wheelchair accessible. I've seen so many builders get caught out because they didn't realise that the laundry also needed to be wheelchair accessible. The laundry must be designed very specifically so someone in a wheelchair can easily access the washing machine and the dryer, and has a minimum one and a half metre turning circle.

Finally, rooming houses need to have several car parks on site, depending on the size, and one of them needs to be designated as a disabled car parking space. But as with the facilities inside, if you don't have a tenant in the property with a disability who is using that car space, one of the other tenants can use it without issue.

These are the main differences between the construction of a rooming house and a traditional house. And these construction issues must all be complied with.

CONSTRUCTION COSTS

Increasing construction costs have been in the media for many years now. The COVID-19 pandemic created disruptions in the supply chain that have not fully returned to normal, and these created a whole bunch of additional challenges. But tools are available that you can use to compare costs so you can be more confident you are comparing apples to apples.

Most people are familiar with cost being discussed as a cost per square metre. But looking at the cost per square metre for a rooming house and the cost per square metre for a normal family home is not comparing apples with apples. As at the time of writing, the cost of a good quality family home is probably around $1800 per square metre. Obviously, that depends on a bunch of things but that's a good ballpark.

But if you are going to build a nine-studio rooming house, the size of the property you'll be looking is artificially small in order to comply with the regulation. As mentioned in chapter 3, investors in Victoria gain significant advantages if the total floor area of all buildings on the land is below 300 square metres. The cost of construction in this instance is around $700,000. But because the size is kept small, the cost per square metre is $2,333—quite a bit more than the $1800 just mentioned. A better way to calculate construction costs, which is used in places such as the United States, is to divide the cost by the number of studios that will eventually be rented, in this case nine. This 'build to rent' methodology would work out as $700,000 divided by nine, which is $77,000 per studio.

Each of these studios will yield anywhere from $230 to $390 per week. I don't know about you, but I haven't seen any properties that you can build for $77,000 that yield those types of returns. Obviously, you still need to add the cost of land, but the overall cost is still a fraction of what a traditional property would cost. And that's the magic of rooming houses.

CHAPTER 7

POST-CONSTRUCTION REGULATION AND BEST PRACTISE

ONCE YOUR ROOMING house has been built, it will be privy to a series of mandatory inspections. You'll also need to register your rooming house with your local council. I run through both these aspects in this chapter. Again, I focus on the requirements in Victoria. All states and territories will have different requirements, so make sure you check the specifics for where your rooming house is located.

INSPECTIONS

The first inspection once your rooming house is complete will be by an authorised officer from the local council, who will check that the property provides the minimum standards of safety and amenity and complies with all local regulations.

In Victoria, a building and fire safety inspection may also be conducted by a qualified fire safety inspector or by Fire Rescue

Victoria or Country Fire Authority, depending on the location of your rooming house. The inspector may look for things such as:

- the general state of repair
- ventilation
- fire hazards
- the prominent display of essential health, building and fire safety measures
- fire prevention systems, including smoke detectors
- emergency lighting and exits
- any other matters that may risk the life, safety or health of anyone using the building.

Legally, rooming houses have an owner and an operator. You as the investor may be both or you may choose to have an operator manage the property for you. I offer this service to investors via my business because managing rooming houses is not as straightforward as managing rental properties, purely because you have so many more tenants and compliance aspects to manage. Outsourcing your management also gives you the option for genuine passive income, where the operator does all the work and then sends through a cheque each month. (More on this in chapter 9.) Whatever route you choose, the operator must keep records of the maintenance of essential safety measures and the current essential safety measures report, because these are likely to be requested during an inspection. Operators face penalties if they do not keep adequate records.

The operator may be issued with a building notice or building order if inspectors believe the rooming house does not comply with building regulations and is, therefore, unsafe.

In addition to the building and fire inspection, an environmental health officer from the local council or the Department of Health, Victoria, will also conduct a health inspection.

Inspectors will be looking at aspects such as the following:

- the register of potential residents
- the number of bathrooms
- general hygiene
- room size
- rubbish collection
- pest control
- adequate supply of hot and cold water.

Again, the operator may be given a written order or notice to carry out work. And this work must be completed before the rooming house is available for potential tenants.

REGISTERING YOUR ROOMING HOUSE

Once the inspections have taken place, you also need to register your rooming house with the local council. This is incredibly important and you face large fines or potential closure if you don't register.

The benefits of registering your rooming house include:

- proof that you are complying with the law and that your performance is monitored regularly by the local council
- access to benefits such as land tax exemptions, if applicable

- the ability for rent from tenants receiving Centrelink payments to be paid via the Centrepay bill paying service, with residents' rent being transferred directly into your bank account
- improving the public image of your rooming house
- helping your case in any hearing with a rent tribunal.

What makes this a little tricky is that not every council has the same registration process, so you will need to speak to staff at your local council, who will be able to tell you what you need to do to comply with legal obligations, council's town planning laws and other requirements.

KEEPING SAFETY INSPECTION RECORDS

Rooming House operators must conduct regular gas and electrical safety checks and make the records available to the authorities and residents on request.

Reminder notifications will also be sent to a rooming house operator periodically to advise them to lodge the required safety check certificates.

The following safety checks are required:

- A gas safety check must be done every two years. Records from these checks, including the compliance certificate and details of the licensed gas fitter who performed the check, must be kept for two years.
- An electrical safety check must be done every two years. Records from these checks, including the compliance certifi-

cate and details of the licensed electrician who performed the check, must also be kept for two years.

For any work performed by a licensed gas fitter or electrician, the rooming house operator must be able to provide a current certificate of compliance.

Once the rooming house is up and running, you may also be subject to visits and inspections. In Victoria, Consumer Affairs Victoria may inspect a rooming house to:

- inform operators and residents of their rights and responsibilities
- ensure that if a resident has paid a bond, it has been lodged with the Residential Tenancies Bond Authority (see the next chapter for more on collecting bonds)
- ensure the rooming house meets minimum standards.

CHAPTER 8

FINDING AND KEEPING GREAT TENANTS

THROUGHOUT THIS BOOK, I've talked about the importance of repositioning rooming houses in the minds of the public and potential tenants. What this looks like on the ground is a new type of tenant from the stereotypical drug dealers and the alcoholics that still sadly spring to mind when some people think about rooming houses.

Several different types of tenants are now attracted to these next-generation rooming houses, often for different reasons. The four main tenant types are:

1. young professionals
2. single retirees
3. students
4. welfare recipients.

YOUNG PROFESSIONALS

These are young, educated working people who are attracted to this solution not just because it allows them to spend more of their income on things other than accommodation but also because it is a low-maintenance solution. They don't want to have to spend their valuable time cleaning a larger home. Everything they need is in the studio while they still have the privacy and independence they want.

Rooming houses are attractive to young couples too as they save toward a deposit on a family home or a great overseas holiday. A rooming house studio just gives them more options.

The advantages of young professionals as tenants are significant. They are working, so paying the rent is rarely a problem. They usually treat their studio well, looking after it and keeping it well maintained. A bonus is that they don't spend much time in the studio because they are either at work or out with friends and family, so there is less wear and tear to the properly. This will keep your maintenance and refurbishment costs down over the long term. When tenants are young professionals, they also help to dispel the stigmas around rooming houses.

The big drawback is that everyone wants young professionals as tenants. At the time of writing, we're still seeing a serious shortage of this type of housing in Australia, so it won't be an issue. But, over time and as supply increases, these tenants will have the pick of the product.

SINGLE RETIREES

These are older people who may have lost a partner, divorced or are otherwise alone later in life. One of the ironies of this group is that they probably fall into the category of baby boomer—who most other generations perceive as being pretty comfortable. Baby boomers were told that they needed to save for retirement, and most do have some assets. The problem with that advice is that it doesn't work, or doesn't go far enough. It may have worked 50 years ago, but the cost of living has increased so much, and people are living so much longer, that it's just not possible to save enough. As a US friend once said to me, these people have realised that they have too much life at the end of their money, rather than too much money at the end of their life.

If a couple divorce, for example, their joint assets, including the family home, are usually sold and divided equally. For many, living more frugally, therefore, becomes a necessity. But it's not just for money reasons that retired singles or even couples opt for this type of accommodation. It's a lifestyle choice where they don't want to have to look after, clean and maintain a large family home. It's also easier to shut the door and leave to go on holiday or visit their kids.

The big advantage of single retirees as tenants is they have almost always owned a home before, so they are respectful of the property and will look after it as though it were their own. As they are retired, they may be in the property more that young professionals but there is still usually less wear and tear than say a studio occupied by either a student or welfare recipient. This is obviously not always the case but as a rule single retirees make great tenants.

They are very similar to young professionals in terms of what they are looking for: a good-quality affordable home that is low maintenance and convenient.

STUDENTS

The great thing about students as tenants is there will always be a steady stream of them to occupy your rooming house, especially if you purposely built the rooming house in the catchment area of a university or training centre. Depending on the student, the course, and the location, you may have students who stay for several years until they graduate or you may have students who only use the accommodation for a certain part of the year. For example, they may live in the rooming house during the academic year and return home for the holidays. In this situation of potentially having studios vacant at certain times of the year, you would need to increase the rent so that you achieve the rent you need during the months they occupy the property. Instead of charging $220 a week for 52 weeks, for example, you may charge $260 for the 44 weeks the studio is rented.

This approach also gives you additional options to make extra money from the property. For example, if the students leave the accommodation for the summer, you could rent the room out to tourists or to meet a short-term rental need for the remaining eight weeks. This is especially relevant if your rooming house is also located near services and local amenities. Students want to be close to their university, but they also want to be near public transport, shops, cafes, clubs and bars so if you've chosen your location accordingly, those amenities may also attract tourists in the summer.

Financially, students can be great tenants but they do come with some risks. Although this isn't true for all students, becoming a student is often the first time they have moved away from home, so they may not be that tidy and can enjoy a good party. The wear and tear is likely to be higher with students than with young professionals or single retirees, for example. As mentioned in chapter 4, students do tend to be a little rowdier, so you may opt to have all studios in the rooming house rented out to students.

Another risk is that you get a student into one of your studios and they end up hating their course and dropping out, and so ending their rental agreement. It can, depending on the time of the year, be quite challenging to get another student into that studio. By the time someone drops out, it's usually a month or so into the course so most other students have already found accommodation.

In this case, you may have to put a different type of tenant into that accommodation, but you would probably need to warn them if it was a house full of students. That said, these rooming houses are not like shared houses—there is a shared kitchen but it wouldn't be very comfortable to have a party in the kitchen! And that's the only shared space—there is no shared living space, for example.

WELFARE RECIPIENTS

This group include all those taken care of by society's safety net. A lot of people in society might need a little help at some point in their lives. In some cases, ill health has meant they have lost their job or they may have been made redundant for other reasons. An unexpected divorce can set people back and they may be looking for affordable accommodation to help them get back on their feet. People end up on benefits and looking for affordable housing for a million reasons, and they are as deserving of a nice home as everyone else.

The big advantage of this type of tenant is that, in many cases, the rent will be paid from the tenant's benefits before it reaches their bank account. In effect, the government is paying the rent. In addition, because you are providing accommodation to mainly low-income residents, in Victoria you may be exempt from paying land tax under the *Land Tax Act 2005*. (You will need to investigate that more thoroughly, and also check the relevant legislation in your jurisdiction.)

The main drawback is that these types of tenants are usually unemployed, hence the benefits, so they tend to spend more time in the studios, which means that wear and tear increases in the property. Welfare recipients can have more behavioural problems than other tenant types but, again, this is a generalisation. There are good and bad tenants in all tenant types, so the key to minimising the risk is to review the applications carefully. Look closely at the behavioural history and check references. This is smart for all tenant types but is especially critical for welfare recipients.

MIXING IT UP

Of course, you can put different tenant types into your property, but you need to stay mindful of the collective vibe. Young professionals and single retirees are often a good mix because they are attracted to this type of property for the same reasons, so they value the same experience.

If you want to offer student accommodation, as mentioned, it may be better to have the whole property dedicated to students because students can be noisy and come and go at odd hours. Young professionals may not mind but single retirees might. It's important to consider who will be a good fit in your property, keeping in mind who else is already in the property.

It's also possible to create a rooming house for a particular group of people who you feel passionate about or an affinity to. For example, I had a client who was passionate about doing something about domestic violence, and they created a rooming house to help female survivors of domestic abuse to get back on their feet and recuperate in peace. We had another client who wanted to create a rooming house for older adults who wanted to downsize or had to downsize because of divorce, and just wanted to live somewhere nice so they didn't run out of money into their old age.

Regardless of how you advertise your rooming house, you must advertise it as a rooming house and not any other type of accommodation. Even though you may be offering something close to a studio apartment, you are not allowed to advertise it that way.

And, of course, it is always wise to have an 'ideal tenant' demographic in mind, right from the start (as discussed in chapter 4). This is just logical because who you plan to accommodate in your rooming house will determine what and where you build. If you want to help welfare recipients, for example, you may opt for a more basic, harder-wearing rooming house on the edges of a town, whereas if you wanted to accommodate students, you would need to find a location within a university catchment area. And if you were aiming to accommodate young professionals or single retirees, you would need to make sure the property was close to their desired amenities.

USING ROOMING HOUSE AGREEMENTS AND BONDS

Whereas a typical rental property will have one tenancy agreement between the owner and the tenant, a rooming house may have five, seven, nine or more rooming house agreements. As I've mentioned, I believe the optimal size is a nine-studio rooming house, in which case you would have nine separate rooming house agreements.

Using formal rooming house agreements isn't mandatory in Victoria, but I always recommend them because this sets the tone of the tenancy and encourages tenants to view their accommodation in the same way they would any other rented house or apartment.

The agreement we use at my business includes the following:

- when the agreement starts
- the address of the property
- the length and type of agreement (fixed term or periodic)
- details, including contact details, for the tenant, the rental provider and their agent (if they have one)
- the amount of the rent, what it includes and how it is to be paid. (In Stone Horizon properties, tenants are charged one fee that covers room rental, electricity, water and internet access.)
- the amount of the bond, if a bond is used
- details of who to contact for urgent repairs
- an option for the tenant and rental provider to say how notices and documents can be delivered
- a summary of the tenant and rental providers rights and obligations
- other terms the rental providers need to follow

Using a tenancy agreement means that once a resident signs a rooming house agreement they are considered a resident under the law, which gives more protections to both the tenant and the owner.

I also encourage the use of bonds in rooming house accommodation for the same reason as a tenancy agreement—it sets the scene. Also, people are very familiar with the idea of paying a bond and this provides extra cover for you as the owner should any repairs be needed once the tenant vacates the property.

The rules around the collection of a bond for a rooming house are, however, slightly different to those for a traditional property. The bond can't be for more than the equivalent of four weeks' rent.

Once you take the bond, in Victoria you must:

- lodge the bond with the Residential Tenancies Bond Authority (RTBA), within two weeks of receiving the bond.
- use the prescribed form (available from rentalbonds.vic.gov.au)
- give the resident a copy of the bond lodgement form
- give the resident two copies of a signed condition report before they move in.

As noted in the final point in the preceding list, if you charge a bond from your resident, you must provide a condition report. You or your operator must complete this condition report with the resident before they move in.

The purpose of this document is to allow the resident and operator to record the room's condition and note any damage that exists in the property before the resident moves in, so they will not be blamed for that damage and potentially lose some of their bond when they move out. This report is then used as evidence down the track by the operator or the tenant to resolve any disputes. For example, the tenant will not be held liable for damage that was identified in the report before they moved in but they may be held liable if new damage is identified once they move out. The condition report also lets the tenant see what condition, including cleanliness, they are expected to leave the property in when their tenancy ends.

The operator must give the resident two completed and signed copies of the condition report. And the resident then has the right to:

- check and add comments to the condition report
- state whether they agree with what the operator has written.

I always recommend that you make sure that each studio is in perfect condition before a new tenant moves in. If that means touching up the paint or filling a dent in a wall, do it. That way everything is clean, undamaged and working.

Once the resident is happy with the condition report, they must sign and give one copy back to the operator within three days of moving into the rooming house. The resident should keep the other copy until the end of their time at the rooming house, and it is the comparison between the condition report at the end of the lease and the condition report at the start of the lease that will determine whether a tenant gets their full bond back.

Even if you decide not to collect a bond, it's worth noting that Consumer Affairs Victoria recommends the use of a condition report. You can find a sample condition report on my website—just go to roominghousemillionaire.com/resources.

WELCOME PACK

There are some rules around what you need to provide to your residents when they start living in your rooming house. To make this easier for tenants and owners at my business, we've created a 'welcome pack' that covers all the mandatory information and some extra useful information relevant to each property.

In Victoria, an operator must give the tenant a copy of the 'Rooming house residents guide'. In addition, if the tenant enters a lease, they must also receive the 'Renters guide'. These guides are available online via the Consumer Affairs Victoria website, where you can also download them in Word format. If you are creating a rooming house in another state or territory, the rules are likely to be similar but make sure you check for your jurisdiction.

The tenant must also be given the operator's full name, address and emergency contact number within seven days of moving in. A written statement outlining the resident's main rights and duties must also be displayed in every resident's room, and given to an occupant no later than the day they agree to start living at the rooming house.

The welcome pack we provide includes these guides and statements, and also includes a set of house rules. The tenant will have been made aware of these rules at the time that they applied to live in the house so this just reminds them. It is also a legal requirement to display the house rules in each room and the common areas.

The house rules usually cover aspects such as the following:

- respecting other residents' right to peace and quiet
- not damaging any property or acting violently
- keeping rooms clean
- not using rooms for illegal purposes.

You can see a copy of the Stone Horizon House Rules at roominghousemillionaire.com/resources.

If an operator wants to make changes to the house rules, they must notify the resident in writing at least seven days before the changes come into effect.

In Victoria, the welcome pack should also include the 'Notice to prospective rooming house resident—exclusive occupancy' form, which explains to the resident that they have an exclusive right to their room. Also include a notice outlining the costs of any extra services the operator provides, if applicable.

CHAPTER 9

MANAGEMENT AND MAINTENANCE

MANAGING A ROOMING house effectively so that you maximise your return on investment is somewhere in-between managing the rental of a normal home and managing a hotel. Let's have a look at why, and how best to manage rooming houses.

DIFFERENT ASPECTS OF ROOMING HOUSE MANAGEMENT

In traditional property investing, if the owner doesn't want the hassle of managing their property, they can off-load it to an agent. The agent will advertise the property, conduct an open house or viewing, collect and check applications, and follow up on references to secure the best tenant at the best price. At least that's the theory. Once the agent hands over the keys to the new tenant, they won't see or interact with the tenant again until the annual property inspection or if an issue arises. The tenant will pay the rent and the agent will take anywhere between 5 and 15 per cent for their trouble.

A rooming house, however, is something quite different. For a start, you usually have nine studios. That means nine viewings, and lots of applications. It is not uncommon for us to organise a viewing over a weekend for a new nine-studio property and get over 50 applications. All those applications need to be checked and we also need to consider the mix of the tenants. Although the tenants are not in a shared house, and they have their own space and independence, you're always wise to put people with similar needs and expectations together. As mentioned in the last chapter, this may mean you largely give the property over to students or create a mix of young professionals and single retirees.

Once the property is built, our clients have the option to take over the management of the property themselves, and we will advise them how best to do that. Or they can opt to have us manage the property for them.

I remember one client who decided to hire a traditional estate agent to manage the property. The problem was that they didn't know how operate a rooming house effectively. Three months later, the client came back to us and explained that in those three months the agent hadn't managed to let any of the rooms. The property had stood empty for three months! We took over the property management and found nine tenants within a couple of weeks.

USING AN AGENT TO MANAGE A ROOMING HOUSE

Like traditional estate agents, we charge a fee based on the property to manage the rooming houses on our list. Whereas the traditional agent charges anywhere from 5 to 15 per cent to manage one tenant in one property, we charge 20 per cent to manage up to nine tenants in nine studios.

Each rooming house we manage for our investors is assigned a property manager. Whereas a traditional agent may manage 300 properties and hope for no issues with most of them on any given week, one of our property managers typically only manages, at most, ten rooming houses. Their role is to not only find a good mix of tenants for each property but also physically visit the property and build relationships to make sure that everyone is happy and settled and to iron out any issues that may arise. This is especially important when new people move in because it may be their first experience of living in a rooming house.

The manager's role also includes co-ordinating the payment of all the utilities and managing the cleaning and maintenance schedule for each property. In the properties we manage, a professional cleaner visits either weekly or bi-weekly and their role is to put the bins out and clean all the common areas. We say in the house rules that everyone must clean up after themselves and make sure that no dishes are left in the sink in the common kitchen, but people are people. By hiring and paying for the cleaning, we ensure that the properties are always in the best possible condition, and this also creates a sense of pride and attachment to the property for the tenants. They can see that the owner and, in turn, us as their agent, are going the extra mile to make this a lovely place to live.

Each agent also visits the property once a month to conduct a general maintenance check. They can then flag anything that needs to be done with our maintenance crew, who will then schedule time to fix the issue. If a wall in a common area is scuffed, for example, someone will come and re-paint that wall. If a door is not closing properly, it will be fixed as soon as it is noticed rather than waiting until the door is hanging off its hinges. It is always better for the tenants and for the owner to fix any issues as soon as they arise. It's better for the tenant because they are reminded that they live in a property where people care, and it's better for the owner because maintenance costs are kept down over the long term. Fixing something when it's a small issue is always more cost effective than waiting until it's a big issue.

In addition, we also conduct a fire safety check every six months. This includes checking all the smoke alarms, fire extinguishers and emergency exit lighting in the building. And, finally, every two years we get an electrician and a plumber to re-certify all the electricity, gas and plumbing.

The property manager will also manage the in-coming and out-going tenants. When someone moves out, the manager will inspect the studio, using the original condition report (covered in the previous chapter) as a guide. Assuming no issues are found, they will authorise the release of the bond. While they are searching for a new tenant, and trying to find someone who will be a good mix with the existing residents, they will organise for the studio to be professionally cleaned. This will include steam cleaning the floor and mattress, checking that everything is in working order and in good condition, and alerting the maintenance crew to any issues that need to be addressed before the new tenant moves in.

You could, of course, carry out all these tasks and manage the property yourself as the property owner. I do, however, recommend that you visit frequently and stay on top of maintenance tasks, as just outlined. A well-maintained property attracts good-quality residents, and helps to keep them in the property for longer.

Most of our clients don't want the hassle of property management or they live out of state, so they prefer for us to take care of everything and simply send them a cheque each month. Although we charge 20 per cent per property, our clients recognise the significant extra value we deliver in keeping their rooming house full and tenants happy. And because we've been doing this for a while now, with many happy tenants, we also have a growing wait list. Often, residents live in a rooming house because it's near a work place such as a hospital but if that person is transferred to another hospital, they often ask us if there is a Stone Horizon rooming house in their next location.

CHAPTER 10

RISK MANAGEMENT STRATEGY

I AM A huge believer in rooming house investing because of the returns that are possible and because of the good that this investment strategy can do in society. Every town and city in the world, and certainly those in Australia, can benefit from the provision of good quality affordable housing. It makes residents lives a little easier and is far superior to the run-down, too expensive property or shared accommodation tenants have been forced to rent in the past.

But every type of investment comes with risk, including rooming houses. The key is to identify those risks and mitigate as many as possible so that you protect your residents and your asset so that everyone wins.

I recommend a five-point plan for risk management:

1. *Be pro-active:* By identifying potential risks early on, you can take steps to mitigate those risks before they become a problem.

2. *Take action:* Identifying the risks is not enough—you
    have to take action to protect your investment and avoid
    legal issues.
3. *Prioritise safety:* Safety of your tenants should
    always come first.
4. *Invest in the future:* By protecting your financial investment
    and keeping up with maintenance and repair, you ensure
    that you stay successful over the long term.
5. *Stay up to date:* By regularly assessing risk and keeping up
    to date with changing regulation you help to mitigate any
    future risk.

With this five-point plan in mind let's unpack some of the risks.

DECREASE IN PROPERTY VALUE

As with all property investing, there is always a risk that the value of
your rooming house will go down. You may remember from chapter
5 that one of the benefits of securing commercial finance over residential finance is that the value of that property is based on the income the
property produces, and not various other factors such as how many
bedrooms there are and how close the property is to good schools.
But there is still an intrinsic value to the overall property, outside of
its ability to get finance.

The best way to mitigate the risk of a decrease in value is to do
thorough due diligence on your location selection process to ensure
that you only invest in areas with clear evidence of capital growth
and strong indicators that growth will continue. This may be a little
confusing, because I've already said that rooming house develop-

ment is not a capital growth strategy and it's not—it's a high cash flow strategy. But when hunting for the ideal location, it's always best to create your rooming house in an area that is experiencing capital growth because it will be easier to find tenants in a growing town or suburb.

Things to look out for that indicate capital growth are:

- *Land supply shortages:* If land shortage is in short supply, clearly people are buying the land—and people tend not to buy land in areas that are going backwards.
- *Multiple, large-scale infrastructure projects:* Investment in infrastructure is a good indication that growth is happening, because local councils and state government see a need for that investment and it is often being driven by an increased population in that area.
- *Location of major employers and industry:* Major employers don't locate to an area unless there is a local workforce.
- *Increasing population:* Linked to all the preceding points, more people moving into an area usually means that area is rising in popularity and offers options for that population, either in housing or employment.
- *Increasing wages:* Increasing wages usually indicate good options for employees, and people not having to leave the area to secure employment is also a good sign.

The key here is to view the property over the long term and not get caught up in value fluctuations. Instead, consider capital growth and the indicators just listed as a sign of the health and attractiveness of the area.

The best way to mitigate this risk even further is to diversify your portfolio of rooming houses across several areas that tick all these boxes. Diversification is a tried and tested risk-management strategy, whether you are investing in shares or rooming houses.

DECREASE IN RENTAL RETURN

A decrease in rental return is probably the most important risk factor to consider for rooming houses. Creating rooming houses is a cash flow strategy so anything that might impact that cash flow is a risk. However, the mitigation for this risk should largely be dealt with when you select the right area. Again, you should only invest in areas where you see evidence of growth and ongoing demand.

Make sure that the location you chose isn't just home to one massive employer or a place that relies on one industry, because you can't control what will happen with that employer or industry and things may change. For example, a large employer may be tempted to relocate to a different state to secure government support. And if they do, your tenant pool just shrunk. Ideally, chose a location that is home to multiple large employers, where many difference industries thrive and with a strong, growing economy.

You need to dig into the demand in the area, rather than just assume demand exists because there is a large employer. For example, we've built up very thorough data sets for every suburb in Victoria that help our clients get a far more nuanced and accurate insight into the real demand in any area. The Australian Bureau of Statistics (ABS) is also a great resource when starting to collect data on any suburb you're considering. Just go to www.abs.gov.au/census/find-census-data/search-by-area and enter the postcode of the suburb.

You'll then be able to access all sorts of information about the residents, including employment type, household composition, and rent and mortgage payments.

If you do find yourself in an area where rents are decreasing, the best protection against that risk is to ensure your rooming house offers above average accommodation so that you still attract the best possible tenants in your area. Also, it's important that you maximise occupancy in your rooming house. It can be easy to get sucked into the old property investing mindset with rooming houses. For example, I've often heard investors talk about how much they are getting for their rooms in the same way they might brag about how much they are getting for their 1-bedroom apartments. But this is the wrong way to look at rooming houses. Focus on the overall return of the property and not necessarily maximising individual rents. If you need to drop the rent on one of your studios to secure full tenancy, do it. The lease types and exact configuration of each studio is usually different anyway so tenants don't necessarily expect that everyone in the building is paying the same rent. It's also very unlikely to come up in conversation because a purpose-built rooming house is not like a shared house where residents mingle and share their lives together all the time.

Aim for maximum occupancy as much of the time as possible. Strong leases of at least three months will also create natural protection against fluctuations in the rental market. If you get enquires from people but don't have any spare rooms, consider creating a waiting list. By the time something comes available that person may have found an alternative rental, but they may know someone else looking for accommodation.

RENTAL VACANCY

Like falling rents, vacancy can throw a spanner in even the best cash flow strategy. But most of this risk can be mitigated by due diligence around site selection and the creation of a good-quality rooming house. Aim for your rooming house to be above the middle of the curve. In other words, if you were to map all the similar accommodation options from worse to best, your rooming house would be above average. When coupled with affordability, you create a winning combination that can naturally protect you from vacancy problems. Nicer, fancier and slicker accommodation options will always be available in your chosen area, but those usually come with a premium price and more cleaning and maintenance commitments, which is not what everyone wants. A lot of the residents in my own rooming houses and those of our clients are not just there because of the affordability. They have chosen the rooming house as a lifestyle choice that is convenient and doesn't require hours of upkeep. They also like the simplicity of one payment that covers rent and utilities. The affordability is almost a bonus.

One of the mistakes I've seen time and time again in rooming house development is investors wanting to stand out, so they make the fixtures and fittings too high end. Even if it's not the investment in drop-down beds and moving walls that I talk about in chapter 6, they will put in quartz worktops or designer bathrooms. But that investment then needs to be paid for, and so the rents become less affordable and more on-par with a traditional studio apartment.

If you find the market for rentals of all types is contracting in your area for whatever reason, the best strategy to mitigate vacancy issues is to set your rent $5 to $10 per week below other similar properties being advertised in your area. This reduction may result in a $260 or $520 per annum loss but it only takes a couple of weeks of a room or studio standing empty to lose that amount anyway, so it's usually worth it.

Again, the key here is to focus on the return of the whole property not individual studios. Part of the beauty of this investment strategy is that you have five or nine studios. If you own a one-bedroom apartment and it's empty for three weeks, it could be disastrous. But if you own a nine-studio rooming house and one of the studios is empty for three weeks, it's not the end of the world because the other eight studios are still delivering revenue. As a 'belt and braces' risk mitigation solution, you could also secure landlord insurance that will cover prolonged vacancy. Although it is harder to secure this type of insurance for rooming houses, we have partnered with insurers to offer this service to our clients.

Finally, the best way to avoid vacancy issues is to create and maintain a great product that people love. I always recommend sending each tenant a little gift, such as chocolates or a magazine subscription, when they renew the lease. It really makes a difference because it converts you from some distant landlord to a human being who cares about your tenants, appreciates them, and wants to say thank you. They are paying your mortgage, after all. Although I wouldn't recommend you mention that in the thank you note!

RISING INTEREST RATES

Here in Australia, and around the world, investors had become very used to low interest rates over the course of the last decade or two, but nothing lasts forever! The risk of rising interest rates has surged to the forefront of risk management for many investors since 2020 as interest rates have climbed back to historical norms.

The best way to mitigate this risks is to employ the services of what we call a 'Top Gun' mortgage broker, ideally one who has experience in helping clients finance rooming houses. This will mean you are always a step or two ahead and will be best placed to refinance or switch to another lender should the rates warrant the switch.

It's also worth pointing out that high-cash-flow strategy of investing in rooming houses is not the same as the buy-to-let strategy of old where investors often end up having to tip in extra money to pay for the mortgage. The old strategy meant that many investors were one interest rate rise away from a heart attack. The rooming house strategy is about creating positive cash flow from the start, so you usually have more wiggle room in the strategy to accommodate rate rises. But it's always smart to keep an eye on the economy, stay in communication with your broker and be ready to switch lender if that makes financial sense.

BAD TENANTS

If you rent out property, having a bad tenant is inevitable at some point in the life of the investment. Often someone will start off as a good tenant but something happens in their lives and the wheels falls off. It might be the end of a relationship or losing a job and that tenant suddenly runs into problems. Inevitably, their problems soon become your problem when behaviour slips or rent is late.

But you can certainly mitigate for a great deal of this risk by having a strong tenant selection process. This means getting a clear picture of who the tenant is and where they work, and taking the time to thoroughly check past rental references. We will refuse would-be tenants if their reference indicated behavioural problems, regular rent arrears or causing damage to the property. We maintain a zero-tolerance policy for misbehaviour—both in terms of assessing their suitability to the property and what we expect from the tenant once they come and live in the property. This means we don't want anyone who abuses alcohol or drugs, and we won't tolerate violence, bullying or intimidation of other tenants, or anyone who consistently breaks the house rules. At times, you will need to evict a tenant. The key is getting it done as quickly and fuss-free as possible.

If you implement an active management strategy, you will also reduce the risks of problems arising or getting worse. Where a normal property investment may have a manager who finds a tenant and hands over the keys, only conducting annual inspections, we advocate a more active approach for rooming houses. The reason is that there is more scope for things to go wrong or people who have not lived in that type of accommodation may have more questions, so we recommend that you or your chosen operator are far more visible in the rooming house. We don't mean you pop in every day, but maybe once a month so that tenants can raise and address issues before they become a bigger problem. Fixing problems when they first arise is always easier—so nip them in the bud. We also recommend regular inspections of the properly, initially every six months so you can make sure they are looking after the property to a high standard.

If a good tenant turns bad, you need to manage them out the property. Any bond held and your landlord insurance can help with any refurbishment that is required to get it rentable again. Also make sure you have a cash buffer to pay for expenses until the insurance pays out.

NATURAL DISASTER

Maybe twenty years ago the risk of natural disasters wasn't as high, but it's something that we all now need to be aware of as extreme weather events happen more frequently. In Australia, the main risks, so far, are fire and flood.

Again, a lot of this risk is mitigated at the site selection stage because you should be looking out for and, in most cases, avoiding a location that is prone to flooding. However, this is not a hard and fast rule. Sometimes the area ticks all the other boxes or it's selling for a great price because of this issue. In this case, you can specifically design and build the property to ensure that it can withstand flood waters with minimal damage. For example, I own a rooming house in an area what is prone to flooding but I deliberately raised the building so it sits on a concrete slab that is about a foot higher than the highest level that flood waters have ever reached in the past 100 years.

Fire is harder to mitigate for but ensuring that the building is built to the highest standard and can withstand earthquake, fire or cyclone is always wise. We don't, for example, invest in Far North Queensland for these reasons—there are just too many extreme events to manage safely.

Regardless of any action you can take during site selection and construction, you also still need to hold building insurance, in case the worst happens. Landlord insurance can also help to cover lost rent while you repair the property. And it's always wise to have a cash buffer to pay for out-of-pocket expenses until the insurance comes through.

PROPERTY FIRE

Here I'm not talking about the risk of bush fires that go crazy, but fire that starts in the property. Statistics from Fire Rescue Victoria show that in the past 10 years, the kitchen was the most common room of fire ignition for non-fatal incidents; however, fires that caused serious injury or death most commonly started in lounge and bedroom areas. The main causes of these fires are:

- cooking left unattended
- misuse of electrical equipment, such as overloading or illegal wiring
- electrical appliances
- smoking.

The first way to mitigate this risk is not to build with materials that are prone to fire or, should fire break out, make the fire worse. This sounds basic and self-explanatory but just think of the Grenfell Tower disaster in London. That building was clad with highly flammable materiel because it looked better and was cheaper than the alternative. When fire broke out on 14 June 2017, it ripped through the building at terrifying speed, killing 72 people. That incident triggered an assessment and replacement of cladding on buildings all over the world, including in Australia.

Beyond taking every precaution possible to limit fire and limit the damage caused by fire, preventing fire from breaking out in the first place is best achieved through house rules (such as no smoking inside the property) and the use of linked smoke detectors. This is mandatory in most states, as are fire extinguishers in common areas and emergency lighting for easier evacuation. The construction of the property should also include insulation that acts as extra fire breaks between the living spaces. These mandatory fire prevention efforts not only keep everyone in the property safer but also ensure quick action should fire break out, which is likely to result in less damage.

Make sure that your properties are inspected regularly by a fire professional who tests the smoke detectors and other safety measures. It's all very well to have them in place, but they need to be tested regularly to make sure they are working properly—otherwise, they are not mitigating your risks. Also, when you or your property manager inspects the property as part of the tenancy agreement, make sure no-one has created a fire hazard in the property, such as by hoarding or having too much in the small space.

Ongoing fire risk is also managed, should the worst happen, via building insurance. As in the earlier risks, landlord insurance may cover lost income while the refurbishment is happening but you may need to use cash buffers until the money comes through.

STRUCTURAL FAULTS

Structural faults are risks associated with the creation of the rooming house. Converting an existing house to a rooming house is always going to come with greater risk because something already exists and that something may be 50 or 100 years old or even older. Structural considerations will need to be taken into account regarding the suitability of the conversion—if, for example, you want to move internal walls. Because of these risks with conversions, and the benefits of purpose-built dwellings I've outlined earlier in the book, I usually recommend you create a purpose-built rooming house because you have a lot more control over the structural integrity of the building.

All our new rooming houses go through formal inspections after the base is created and then again once the frame is up.

Whatever you decide to do, a great deal more structural risk can be mitigated by engaging a specialist builder with a proven track record. If your builder has created rooming houses in the past, you should be able to see those rooming houses, either in person or via video walk-through. It's important to recognise that building a rooming house is not the same as building a block of flats or a family home. And make sure you get a copy of the inspection report from the building surveyor to confirm structural compliance.

And, finally, you should also be provided with a builder's warranty and structural guarantee. When we build rooming houses for investors, we provide a 10-year warranty that ensures we will fix any defects that occur within the first 10 years. This is longer than most warranties but we have never had a structural fault in any of the properties we've built. Be sure you get a warranty that covers at least the first seven years.

PEST INFESTATION

Pest infestation is a risk but it's certainly less of a risk with a purpose-built rooming house than a conversion. If you are converting, you will need to have a professional inspection to make sure nothing untoward is lurking behind any walls or under any floors. For a new build, there isn't the same risk.

The best way to manage this risk going forward is to maintain a cash buffer should you need any pest extermination, but this can be further prevented by regular property inspection so that you or your property manager can be alerted to any issues that may create an infestation—for example, if the hygiene of the property is not up to scratch. In addition, you should have a regular regime of professional pest inspections for the property in place, and any advice from the professional should be followed.

BUILDER GOING BUST DURING THE BUILD

The risk of your builder going bust has been rising in urgency over the last couple of years with more and more investors either being burnt or hearing horror stories that make them nervous.

The first way to mitigate this is to choose a proven, reputable builder that is not showing any signs of financial distress. This is obviously not that easy to find out yourself but some signs are easier to spot—if a company has a reputation for paying their bills late, for example, best to steer clear. In Victoria, you can also use the Victorian Building Authority (VBA) 'Find a practitioner' tool to find out more details about your proposed builder. You can search using the builder's name or registration number and check if their license has ever been suspended or cancelled, or if they have been placed on VBA's Disciplinary Register. Just go to www.vba.vic.gov.au/tools/find-practitioner. Other states and territories offer similar licence searches, so check your jurisdiction.

The next obvious step is to never authorise a payment until you have evidence that the work has been done. If you are paying in stages, the relevant stage should be complete before you part with your money. For example, we do this in a very open and transparent way and it's automated. Each client gets access to a project management system, and in that system we include a link to a photo album where we put regular photos of what is happening on site. We don't issue a progress claim invoice until we have added the right set of pictures and documentation that proves that the work related to the progress claim invoice has been completed and not only completed but also done to a standard beyond the building code. We also add the inspection reports as they are completed, so the investor has all the evidence that their rooming house is progressing well. There is no mystery with our building. You won't have to send a thousand emails to get a response and you won't have to trust that when the builder says something is done that it is done. We provide evidence all the way along. This is the standard you should expect from your builder and/or project manager.

You can also take certain steps to prevent the worst from happening. Before construction starts, you can get your builder to issue a certificate of insurance to you as the investor. If you become a client of Stone Horizon, this means that should something happen to us the bank will enforce the insurance. According to the insurance policy, the insurer working with the bank will allocate a replacement builder to complete the project. We pay for that insurance ourselves as a 'belt and braces' risk mitigation to allay any lingering fears a client may have about our business. For the record, no-one has ever used the insurance.

BUILDER GOES OVER CONTRACT DATE

Your builder going over your contract date is the last risk in what has deliberately been a very comprehensive list. Again, the best way to mitigate this risk is to choose a builder that has a proven track record. This building industry has seen significant challenges since the COVID-19 pandemic, with some builders running into problems in the supply chain. We have changed some of our internal processes to try to better accommodate these issues because projects running over costs money and we are keen to avoid that as much as possible for us and our clients.

For us, we are as keen as the investor to keep the project on track because this allows us to start the next rooming house faster or to move the project into the property management phase. To further protect the investor, ensure your contract includes a clause around liquidated damages. So, for example, if an investor chooses Stone Horizon to build their rooming house, we as the builder are financially penalised if anything under our control goes over time. And the more we go over the agreement, the bigger the fine. This fine can then help you as the investor with the loan servicing costs that you will still need to meet until the project is up and running and full of happy tenants.

The key to risk management—for all potential risks—is to be ahead of the game and anticipate and mitigate as many risks as possible through the strategies outlined in this chapter. This approach provides a robust safety net should anything go wrong.

CHAPTER 11

CASE STUDIES

BY NOW, I hope you are excited about investing in rooming houses. This is a strategy that not only genuinely helps people to live in good-quality affordable housing but also is a game changer when it comes to creating positive cash flow for the here and now. It's time to puts some numbers and stories to the theory so you can see just what's possible.

The case studies provided here are all real stories; the only thing I've changed is the names.

PROPERTY #1

This client, let's call her Julie, owned a property in Melton. She had bought it several years before we met and had been renting it out. As is so often the case, the rent didn't quite cover the mortgage so she had some additional costs each year but was confident that in the long run it would be a good investment. Julie would have almost certainly kept the property and continued with her strategy had the property not burnt down. Fortunately, no-one was hurt and Julie had insurance.

The property itself, however, was beyond salvation and needed to be flattened and rebuilt.

During this time when her claim was being processed, she heard about rooming houses and Stone Horizon. In her situation, the insurance company was not going to rebuild the house but instead was going to give her a cheque. Once the house was flattened, what was left was a large block of land in Melton, and Julie was keen to explore her options about how best to utilise the block.

We had a meeting and she soon realised that she had an opportunity to build something different that could work harder for her and meet a growing need in the area. She decided to create a purpose-built nine-studio rooming house. Her costs are listed in the following table. The land price and stamp duty listed were what she paid for the property several years before.

Acquisition	
Land price	$450,000
Stamp duty	$22,070
Land transfer	$1,148
Legals	$1,000
Adjustments	$1,500
Design and engineering	$29,500
Construction cost	$700,000
Total cost	**$1,205,218**

Once the property was designed, it took just over six months to build and Julie transformed a negatively geared rundown house into a positive cash flow rooming house. Julie decided that she didn't want to manage the property herself and so, once it was built, Stone Horizon took over the management. Within about a week and a half all the studios were rented, each for $270 a week, giving an annual rental income of $126,360.

Julie's additional expenses are included in the following table.

Rental	Size	Rent per week	Annual
Income	9	$270	$126,360
Expenses			
Rates and insurance			-$4,000.00
Utilities			-$7,500.00
Repairs and maintenance			-2,000.00
Property management		20%	-$25,272.00
Land tax			-$1,769.50
		Net Rent	**$85,819**

Of course, like most people Julie didn't have a spare $1,205,218 down the back of her couch to cover total costs. (Because the property was bought some time ago, Julie had paid off some of the original mortgage. But to keep this case study closer to most people's situation, I've included the full original cost of the land and stamp duty in her costings.) So Julie needed to secure finance, and did so via a residential loan at 70 per cent LVR to build the rooming house at a rate of 4 per cent. The cheque she received from the insurance company along with some savings covered the 30 per cent cash she needed to secure the loan.

Finance	
Finance	70%
Interest rate	4.00%
Financed amount	$805,000.00
Cash required	$400,218.00
Loan payments	$32,200.00
Net cash flow	**$53,619**

Performance	
Yield	10.48%
Net cash flow	$53,619
% Return on cash	13.40%

Julie's net cash flow on that single property is $53,619 per year ($126,360 income—($40,541 expenses + $32,200 loan repayments)). We manage the property for her and bank transfer the money directly into her account every month—and she will continue to receive that money for the rest of her life (unless, of course, she sells the property.

Julie was so thrilled with the results that she decided to take another property in her portfolio and convert it to a rooming house. Unlike the first one, which had been damaged by fire, this particular property was just a little rundown. She demolished it and we built a rooming house for her instead. And her long-term aim is to repeat the process for all the remaining properties in her portfolio so she will eventually end up with seven rooming houses. And each complete rooming house helps her to fund the next one.

It's also worth pointing out that this strategy has completely changed her life. Julie's in her early 60s, works in health care and has worked incredibly hard for decades. Part of the issue for her had been that she had this portfolio of properties that were supposed to deliver financial freedom but instead required her to work overtime to subsidise them. Now she can see a way out. Once she has the seven rooming houses, each creating positive cash flow, she will be able to either retire or go part-time. Julie loves her job and gets a lot of satisfaction from it but it was not fun when she was having to routinely work 60 hours a week. Rooming houses will deliver the financial freedom she was hoping for when she got into property in the first place.

PROPERTY #2

The second case study was a smaller rooming house, built on one of the ugliest blocks of land imaginable! This client was 'Alan'. Alan was in his mid-30s and had worked his way up to consultant in one of the big firms. He made good money but he also enjoyed spending it and had only managed to save $160,000. He was now married with two young kids and realised that he needed to get smart about how to make that $160,000 really work for him and his family and give him more income options. We had a chat and we tailored a solution for him based on the resources he had available.

With any new land development, anywhere, the developer will release the sale in stages. And in these new developments, the nice square or rectangle blocks sell first and then there are a couple of less symmetric blocks that don't sell. The developer doesn't worry about those and instead pushes on and opens the next stage for sale. Again, the nice square or rectangular blocks sell out, leaving behind a couple of ugly ducklings. By the time the development is up and running, the developer is still holding those ugly duckling plots—and now highly motivated to sell and is often prepared to discount. That's what happened in this case. We found one of those ugly duckling plots in a development in metro Melbourne. This site just could not have worked for a traditional family home, but our design team were able to make it work for a five-studio rooming house.

And that's what we built for Alan. Because the plot was unusual, it was still a bargain for metro Melbourne. All acquisitions costs are shown in the following table.

Acquisition	
Land price	$250,000
Stamp duty	$10,070
Land transfer	$680
Legals	$1,000
Adjustments	$1,500
Design and engineering	$29,500
Construction cost	$570,000
Total cost	**$862,750**

The rental income and running costs for this five-studio rooming house are outlined in the following table.

Rental	Size	Rent per week	Annual
Income	9	$310	$80,600
Expenses			
Rates and insurance			-$3,700.00
Utilities			-$5,980.00
Repairs and maintenance			-$328.00
Property management		20%	-$16,120.00
Land tax			-$1,019.50
		Net Rent	$53,453

Because Alan still had a very good job, he was able to secure a residential mortgage to build the property and he used his savings and did some overtime to cobble together $165,750. The finance costs are shown in the following table.

Finance	
Finance	85%
Interest rate	4.00%
Financed amount	$697,000.00
Cash required	$165,750.00
Loan payments	$27,880.00
Net cash flow	$25,573

Performance	
Yield	9.34%
Net cash flow	$25,573
% Return on cash	15.43%

This single strategy gave Alan an immediate cash injection every year of $25,573.

PROPERTY #3

The third case study comes from 'Mark'. Like Julie, he already owned a portfolio of properties, only his was significant. It had taken him over 20 years to accumulate these properties and some were now creating positive cash flow although most were not. The positive cash flow properties were helping to offset those that were not yet paying for themselves.

Mark also chose to build a nine-studio rooming house, only he chose to build in regional Victoria. His acquisition costs are shown in the following table.

Acquisition	
Land price	$280,000
Stamp duty	$11,870
Land transfer	$750
Legals	$1,000
Adjustments	$1,500
Design and engineering	$29,500
Construction cost	$700,000
Total cost	**$1,024,620**

Like with Julie, we designed and built the rooming house for Mark in around six months, and Mark then asked us to manage it. The rental income and costs are included in the following table.

Rental	Size	Rent per week	Annual
Income	9	$260	$121,680
Expenses			
Rates and insurance			-$4,000.00
Utilities			-$7,500.00
Repairs and maintenance			-$2,000.00
Property management		20%	-$24,336.00
Land tax			-$1,132.00
		Net rent	**$82,712**

Of course, it cost money to create this asset and while the cost of buying the property was significantly cheaper in region Victoria Mark still needed to secure finance to finish the build (and you'll see his interest rate is higher, due to RBA increases). Those finance costs are shown in the next table.

Finance	
Finance	70%
Interest rate	5.20%
Financed amount	$686,000.00
Cash required	$338,620.00
Loan payments	$35,672.00
Net cash flow	**$47,040**

Performance	
Yield	11.88%
Net cash flow	$47,040
% Return on cash	13.89%

What was especially heartwarming about Mark's story was that as soon as the rooming house was complete and fully rented, he was able to quit his job—something he had been desperate to do for years. Mark was a very senior executive in a large company and the pressure and demands of the job were significant. And at times he hated it. But something really odd happened when he was finally in a position where he could quit … he decided to stay. His whole outlook and attitude changed because he had real freedom. He wasn't forced to stay because he needed the money to pay for his properties anymore; instead, he was choosing to stay—knowing all the time that if the day ever came when he felt he'd had enough, then he could resign and move into the next phase of his life.

PROPERTY #4

Our final case study is from 'Maggie'. In her late 50s when I met her, Maggie was divorced with two grown up sons. In the divorce settlement, she kept the family home in Sydney and her ex-husband received other assets. It was a lovely home but it didn't give her any income, and so she decided to sell it and use the money to buy a campervan and buy land and build a rooming house in Victoria with her two sons.

The campervan would be her home and she could travel or visit friends and family. At the same time, she would receive an income from the rooming house that would be more than enough for her needs, especially as she no longer had a large family home to take care of and maintain. To Maggie, this strategy gave her the financial freedom she wanted on her terms—and would go on providing income for her sons long after she was no longer around. Maggie's acquisition costs are shown in the following table.

Acquisition	
Land price	$110,000
Stamp duty	$1,670
Land transfer	$352
Legals	$1,000
Adjustments	$1,500
Design and engineering	$29,500
Construction cost	$720,000
Total cost	**$864,022**

Maggie's rental income and costs are shown in the following table.

Rental	Size	Rent per week	Annual
Income	9	$230	$101,430
Expenses			
Rates and insurance			-$4,000.00
Utilities			-$7,500.00
Repairs and maintenance			-$328.00
Property management		20%	-$20,286.00
Land tax			-$494.50
		Net rent	**$68,821**

Maggie financed the project without the involvement of a lender, so she achieved a higher net cash flow of $68,821.

CONCLUSION

I'VE ALWAYS BELIEVED that property is a fantastic way to create and build wealth, but the traditional strategies just don't work anymore. Life is stressful enough without having to constantly top up mortgage payments or cover additional costs of property that is negatively geared.

We are also in the middle of a housing crisis that is showing no signs of abating. If anything, it will continue to get worse. The boom and bust of residential property makes finding a good investment and finding a good rental home increasingly challenging for millions of people.

Rooming houses are the solution. Not only does their creation genuinely help people to live better, more enjoyable lives but they also deliver an envious return on investment. It's a win–win. The tenant gets a lovely, clean, albeit small affordable home that suits their needs without any of the hassle, and the investor gets positive cash flow for the rest of their lives.

I hope I've opened your eyes to the possibilities. Good luck, and please get in touch as you start out on your journey. Reach out if you have any questions, and I'd also love to hear about any successes you have along the way. If you'd like some extra help and more guidance on what's possible for your budget, contact us at Stone Horizon to set up a discovery call.

Get in touch via the following:

Email: henryv@stonehorizon.com.au
Website: www.stonehorizon.com.au
Phone: 1300 31 07 06
Facebook: www.facebook.com/hvila
LinkedIn: www.linkedin.com/in/henry-vila/
Instagram: www.instagram.com/henryvila.au/

www.ingramcontent.com/pod-product-compliance
Lightning Source LLC
Chambersburg PA
CBHW040857210326
41597CB00029B/4884